To: _____

From: _____

TEACHING FOR GOD'S GLORY

Daily Wisdom and Inspiration for New Teachers

Tyler Harms

ELM HILL

A Division of
HarperCollins Christian Publishing

www.elmhillbooks.com

Teaching for God's Glory
Daily Wisdom and Inspiration for New Teachers

Published in Nashville, Tennessee, by Elm Hill, an imprint of Thomas Nelson. Elm Hill and Thomas Nelson are registered trademarks of HarperCollins Christian Publishing, Inc.

Elm Hill titles may be purchased in bulk for educational, business, fund-raising, or sales promotional use. For information, please e-mail SpecialMarkets@ThomasNelson.com.

Scripture quotations marked ESV are from the ESV® Bible (The Holy Bible, English Standard Version®). Copyright © 2001 by Crossway, a publishing ministry of Good News Publishers. Used by permission. All rights reserved.

Scripture quotations marked GNT are from the Good News Translation in Today's English Version—Second Edition. Copyright 1992 by American Bible Society. Used by permission.

Scripture quotations marked GW are from *God's Word*®. Copyright © 1995 God's Word to the Nations. Used by permission of Baker Publishing Group. All rights reserved.

Scripture quotations marked NCV are from the New Century Version®. © 2005 by Thomas Nelson. Used by permission. All rights reserved.

Scripture quotations marked NIV are from the Holy Bible, New International Version®, NIV®. Copyright © 1973, 1978, 1984, 2011 by Biblica, Inc.® Used by permission of Zondervan. All rights reserved worldwide. www.Zondervan.com. The "NIV" and "New International Version" are trademarks registered in the United States Patent and Trademark Office by Biblica, Inc.®

Scripture quotations marked NKJV are from the New King James Version®. © 1982 by Thomas Nelson. Used by permission. All rights reserved.

Scripture quotations marked THE MESSAGE are from *The Message*. Copyright © by Eugene H. Peterson 1993, 1994, 1995, 1996, 2000, 2001, 2002. Used by permission of NavPress. All rights reserved. Represented by Tyndale House Publishers, Inc.

Library of Congress Cataloging-in-Publication Data

Library of Congress Control Number: 2019912956

ISBN 978-1-400327485 (Paperback)
ISBN 978-1-400327751 (Hardbound)
ISBN 978-1-400327492 (eBook)

DEDICATION

To my beautiful bride and best friend, Christina.
Thank you for your overflowing love and support.

TABLE OF CONTENTS

BEFORE THE YEAR BEGINS

Think about what a friendly, student-owned room looks like and let the students "decorate" their space. Their fingerprints should be everywhere! (This takes much of the pressure off the teacher as well!) Websites like Pinterest, etc. have many great ideas to liven up a classroom. I have put many posters up at the beginning of the year, but it is the students' work that helps to make your room feel like their own.

You can also go back to the activities on your wall throughout the year to build background knowledge on new content that you are learning in class. There will be many students in your class that are very creative and others that are not. Involve all of your students in some way to make them feel like they are a part of the class. Create a wall of fame of some sort to display student work and/or information about the student. Some classes have a "Student of the Week", which involves students sharing some information about themselves and so everyone can get to know them. Afterward, the student can put their information on the wall so everyone can read it throughout the year.

Send letters to the students welcoming them to your class. Invite them to visit their classroom. Kids love getting letters and postcards in the mail. If you have a little bit of time in the summer, write a short note or send a postcard to your students. Tell them that you are excited about having them in your class and maybe give them some details about how your summer is going. Reach out to the students and parents with a positive greeting. Students will remember the kind gesture.

There will be some students that may benefit from a tour of the school and/or your classroom before the year begins. I always encouraged students that I worked with (students with an IEP) to come visit the school to walk around and get a feel of the classroom and the building. Offer a map of the school to help orient them around the building. The parents and students will be very appreciative of you taking the extra time to get to know their child.

Make sure you have the essentials and a safe environment. Look over your IEPs to see if you need to have your room configured in a certain way. We had a few students who used motorized wheelchairs so it was necessary to have adequate space for them to access class materials. Have different areas in your room designated for different purposes. You may want to have your turn-in basket by the front door so students can turn in their work when they enter the classroom. In my groups, I have a bucket with essential items in them. I usually have tape, colored pencils, sticky notes, scissors, markers, a calculator, and a ruler. I have found that this helps cut down on transition time when the materials are right there in front of the students. No matter how you design your class, make sure you have your curriculum ready to go as well!

Create a classroom setup that lets systems run themselves; that way you can concentrate on the most important people in the room – the students and their families. Get to know both groups, and your year will be much more successful. Let the students do the talking for you! Have students work collaboratively in groups and give each student a job in the group. For example, a student could be a manager, timer, recorder, or spokesperson. You could rotate these jobs each week, so each student has a turn. There are many online programs such as Google Classroom, Schoology, etc., that are great learning management systems (LMS) to help students manage their own assignments and keep track of work.

There is always work to be done in the classroom, and the students should help to allow it to run smoothly. The class should be student-run so putting things into place to allow students to have ownership of the classroom is essential. Some students can be in charge of passing out papers and stuffing Friday Folders, and all students can and should help you clean up the room at the end of the day. The custodians will much appreciate it!

Complete any compliance work in the summer (bloodborne pathogens, etc.). There are some nuts and bolts housekeeping type of items that you may want to get out of the way before school starts. After you are hired, ask your administrator about any certifications you may need to start the year. Frequently a new teacher will need to be CPR/first aid certified. Also, if you are a special educator, you will most likely need to be trained in Crisis Prevention Intervention (CPI) training. This is an eight-hour or so training, so by doing this in the summer you will not have to be absent from school during the first part of the year.

Usually, this compliance work such as bloodborne pathogens, concussion, etc., that is provided by the district is online a week or two before school starts. I usually watch the videos and answer the questions while I am at home and have some extra time. You could even sit outside in the sun and do it! Completing the requirements early may be helpful and eliminate some stress. There will most likely be some other new teacher orientation as well, so trying to organize all of that in the summer will help you to have a better start to the year.

A Classroom Prayer for the New School Year[1]

Powerful and almighty God, You are so amazing! You've had a plan for these children since before time began, and you've always known that our lives would cross paths this year.

Please give me the gift of discernment to understand their needs and how I can meet them. Show me everything I need to know to teach these little ones and develop the gifts that you've given them. Let my enthusiasm be evident every day because my joy doesn't come from having a perfect classroom, it comes from knowing You. Jesus, I pray that you would fill me with your strength and perfect peace each morning and carry me throughout each day.

Put a genuine smile on my face and help me to be as patient and loving with these children as You have been with me.

Remind me that this job is a privilege and that I am fulfilling Your call on my life by showing up in this classroom each day.

Surround me with supportive, positive influences and help me to speak only truth and light so that my colleagues and supervisors will consistently see You in me.

I dedicate this classroom to You: let Your name triumph over any negativity and may everything that happens here brings glory to Your name.

I thank you for giving me Your holy Word so that I have a place to turn when I need to be uplifted.

Thank you for filling me with the passion and enthusiasm that can only come from having God within'.

May Your name be glorified in everything that happens here as Your mercies are made new each morning.

AMEN

---

[1] Angela Watson, "Who's in Charge Here?" The Cornerstone Devotions for Teachers, accessed June 21, 2019, http://devotions.thecornerstoneforteachers. com/2006/08/whos-in-charge-here.html. Used by permission.

First Quarter

(AUGUST-OCTOBER)

DAY 1

Start children off on the way they should go,
and even when they are old, they will not turn from it.

Proverbs 22:6 NIV

Make your first week of school about getting to know your students, developing relationships, and the classroom routine. Students tend to learn better and be more cooperative when they feel known at school. You have to go slow to move fast later in the year. The first few weeks of school should be used to get to know your students, practice routines, and solidify expectations for the classroom.

Use this time at the beginning of the year to have some fun with your students. Try some team building activities such as the human knot, relay races, etc., to help build a sense of community in the classroom. Move these activities into your content areas and discuss how to work in collaborative groups. Do not assume that students know how to do this well. If you want students to work in groups throughout the year, take time to practice how this will run and how students should communicate with one another that is respectful. So much is going on at this time of the year, but once you get to know your students and they know your routines, you will be ready to hit the ground running in your content areas.

DAY 2

Listen to advice and accept discipline, and at the end, you will be counted among the wise. Many are the plans in a person's heart, but it is the Lord's purpose that prevails.

PROVERBS 19:20–21 NIV

Administrators will not always have time to answer every question you have. Ask for and utilize a mentor. Good mentors will listen to you when your day has been horrible, give you "veteran teacher advice," introduce you to staff members, and review school and district-wide policies.

Your mentor can also help you with little things such as how to set up your gradebook, copy machines, etc. Mentors will also give you insight into the culture of the building as well as any advice about working with staff members. They can also help with your curriculum planning and pacing guides. Make sure to buy your mentor some coffee, or give a simple thank you note for helping you out.

DAY 3

*The Father has loved us so much that we are called
children of God. And we really are his children.*

1 John 3:1 NCV

Build those relationships right away. Get to know your students by learning about their interests as well as their likes and dislikes. This helps so much in understanding how to teach them. The beginning of the year might be a good idea to have a fun activity like a student survey or a student of the week, which gives students a platform to share their stories with the rest of the class.

Try any incentives you may have throughout the year and work with the students who have behavior plans. Speak with the school social worker, special education provider, and/or parents to see how to best implement the behavior plan. Your colleagues have a wealth of knowledge and can help you adjust as necessary.

Students get a fresh start each year, and we should give that student a chance. Summer can be a time for students to grow and mature and they often surprise us when they return in the fall. It is always good to be prepared.

DAY 4

We are God's workers, working together.

1 CORINTHIANS 3:9 NCV

Y ou have made it past the first week! What went well? What did not go so well? Even if you do not have a lot of time after the first week of school, try making it a priority to write some things down that you can build from for next year. Talk with colleagues to find out what went well for them during the first week of school and what areas they might modify.

Our grade level team looked back at the sixth-grade orientation in the first week and talked about, as a grade level, what went well and what things we can do differently. It was great to see all of the teachers' perspectives come together to help each other. It may be beneficial to do this for each week. This will give you some insight for the next school year on what changes should be made, what you can build in, or what things could be taken out because your students may already know the material.

DAY 5: REFLECTION AND PRAYER

DAY 6

People harvest only what they plant.

GALATIANS 6:7 NCV

Remember to prioritize the most critical aspects of teaching, which are your individual student needs (504s, IEPs, etc.), and how you will deliver your curriculum. Look over your curriculum scope and sequence to see where you can connect to other content areas. This is great at the middle and high school levels because you can help reinforce content-specific vocabulary and have students writing across the curriculum. This also lends itself more to project-based learning, which is more fun than worksheets. Here are the top three priorities to keep in mind when starting the school year:

1. Get to know your students (IEPs, gifted, emotional support, etc.).
2. Decide how you are going to implement your curriculum and schedule (rules, routines, emergency situations, etc.).
3. Set up your classroom. I used to be so concerned with #3, but quickly learned that if #1 and #2 are not in place, your class will not run as smoothly as expected. Probably the easiest thing to do and the most fun is setting up your classroom.

DAY 7

*Don't let anyone look down on you because you are young,
but set an example for the believers in speech, in conduct,
in love...and in purity.*

1 TIMOTHY 4:12 NIV

It is important in the first week to set the tone for the school year. You are in charge of their education; their parents trust you to take care of their children throughout the day. It is our responsibility to provide all students with an environment that is conducive to learning. Stay firm and consistent with the rules you have all agreed upon. Students will respect you more if you are consistent and abide by the social contract you have created together.

I was having a conversation with a teacher once and she asked me, "How come my kids are always out of control in the afternoon?" I worked with her during the morning in her math class, and her students knew expectations, followed the structure of the lesson, and the teacher was consistent. In the afternoon, students had more freedom and often tested the limits of the social contract. The teacher, possibly tired from the day herself, backslid a little on the consistency piece of the social contract, and that is when the problems started. Be firm but kind at the start of the school year. Be consistent and they will respect you for the rest of the year.

DAY 8

Each of us is an original.

GALATIANS 5:26 THE MESSAGE

S pend time getting to know your students. This can be time spent on fun games, student essays, a student of the week, etc. No matter what grade level you teach, you can always talk about good things that are happening in the students' lives. If you teach at the middle school or high school levels, you definitely will not have enough time to go through every single student to share good things that are happening with them. You may have to catch up with other students in the hallways during passing periods or during work time. Try to make some sort of connection with every student in your class.

For elementary and upper elementary school teachers, there is more time in your day for this. Some teachers like to do it right away in the morning after announcements, or while they are filling in their planners; others want to do it after lunch to help the students settle back into the routine of school. It might be a good idea to have a timer, or something similar, to keep you on track for when you need to get back into the content. It is just refreshing for everyone to have a little brain break and to talk about something that is not school related.

DAY 9

Anxiety weighs down the heart, but a kind word cheers it up.
Proverbs 12:25 NIV

C all each parent during the first month of school. If you are at the elementary level or a special education teacher, you may have a specific class list or caseload to work with. You will be able to access the phone numbers and/or email addresses of the students' parents in your grade book system. This can be a quick conversation to find out if the parents have any questions or concerns. This is also a time when you can communicate to the parents one or two things that you already appreciate about your child. It is just a great thing to have the first phone call from the school be a positive one to start the year.

I have had many parents say that this may be the first positive phone call they have received for their child at school. The rest of the year may be pretty rough for their child, but setting the tone and opening the gates for communication on a positive note will be helpful in the long run. Parents will see that you are there for their child and will let you know when things are going well, and when their child is struggling in the classroom. If you teach middle school or high school, you might have many students that you work with during the day. It may not be realistic to call every single parent in the first month of school, but trying to contact parents whose student may struggle in your class is an excellent way to start the year off on a positive note.

DAY 10: REFLECTION AND PRAYER

DAY 11

My dear brothers and sisters, take note of this: Everyone should be quick to listen, slow to speak, and reluctant to become angry...

James 1:19 **NIV**

Within the first weeks of school, try and get an overview of each unit in your content area(s). Find a department colleague to help you see the big picture of the unit and how to read the teacher's guide. It might be a good idea to look at any summative assessments and/or projects for the unit so that you know what learning targets are essential. Try to plan ahead with curriculum and your school year, but sometimes it is helpful to take it a week at a time, or even a day at a time. It is easy to get overwhelmed and put too much on your plate.

You will have some weeks when you can barely get through the day and others when you feel like you have a little extra time. Use those weeks to glance ahead and plan out your lessons. Grade level teams often have weekly meetings to help plan lessons and make copies for the next week's lessons. Make sure you get in touch with your colleagues to know when those meetings are scheduled. This is also a great time to bounce some ideas around regarding new lessons to try with your students.

DAY 12

Then, because so many people were coming and going that they did not even have a chance to eat, he said to them, "Come with me by yourselves to a quiet place and get some rest."

MARK 6:31 NIV

The teachers' lounge is a good place to eat and get to know your colleagues a little better. Students also are vying for your time at lunch to hang out, play some games, or get away from their own busy lunchroom. I typically eat lunch in my room because I always have students coming in to catch up on missing work or just to relax and hang out.

Make sure you use this time to recharge. Pack a healthy lunch that will sustain you throughout the day. It is nice every once in a while to go out to eat. It allows you to get some fresh air! As a first-year teacher, you will have a big learning curve ahead of you, and your colleagues will understand if you have to get some things done to prepare for your next class. Keep a jar of chocolate around for you and other staff who need a pick-me-up after lunch!

DAY 13

Fathers, do not exasperate your children; instead, bring them up in the training and instruction of the Lord.

EPHESIANS 6:4 NIV

B uild class culture with routines and expectations to help build consistency for students throughout the year. During the first few months, create a class culture that can demonstrate appropriate behaviors in all areas of the building. Have students model and give examples of what correct behavior looks like. Also, what are the routines with class work? Expectations and routines look different in each classroom. If you teach multiple subjects then you will want to review the procedures and classroom norms with your students. Having the students be a part of the process will allow students to take ownership of how their classroom is run.

Create a social contract that helps keep teachers and students accountable for creating a culture that is safe, productive, and accepting of all ideas. One way to do this is by using large piece of paper and having the students list what is expected of the students and teacher throughout the day. The following are examples of expectations that could be included in the list: being respectful, being kind to others, and giving feedback quickly. Then you can make copies for the students or leave it as a poster and have all students sign it. This will be a reminder throughout the year of the expectations contract everyone is agreeing to. Come back to the social contract early and often throughout the year. Start each day by going over it with your students, and have students act out examples using the social contract. It is pretty funny to watch them do examples of undesirable behavior!

DAY 14

Jesus said, "Let the little children come to me, and do not hinder them, for the kingdom of heaven belongs to such as these."

MATTHEW 19:14 NIV

I first taught in a school where there was a vast difference in the students' socio-economic statuses. Many of our students were living below the poverty line, and in some cases were homeless, living in hotels, and sometimes cars. Take a few minutes and get to know where your students are coming from to get a better idea of what their needs are. Talk to the school counselor or previous year's teacher to get some advice.

Some students have to overcome many obstacles just to get to school every day, and knowing this as a teacher will help better prepare you for one of those students who comes to see you in the morning. I always thought students had a morning routine similar to mine. I would get up, take a shower, eat some breakfast, brush my teeth, and head out to work. Many of these students do not even have food or water turned on at home because they cannot afford to pay the bills. Take the time to get to know the needs of your students and pass that information on to the school social workers to find available resources to help them.

DAY 15: REFLECTION AND PRAYER

DAY 16

"If you believe, you will get anything you ask for in prayer."
MATTHEW 21:22 NCV

G et in contact with each parent to introduce yourself, and invite them to contact you regarding anything concerning your student. Become partners with the parents. There will be many ways in which you can have parents be active in your classroom. Let parents know how they can access their child's grades. You can do this yourself or send them to the front office where can assist them in getting alerts when their grades drop or if there are missing assignments.

It is also a great idea to ask for volunteers for your classroom. I realize that this is more common in elementary schools, but middle and high school teachers have nothing to lose by asking for some volunteers to read tests aloud to students. They could come an hour or two a week to help tutor a struggling math student, or just to be a positive mentor for a student who is having a hard time. Budgets are tight and finding extra support in your room will be so helpful when you have a stack of papers to hand back and copies to make. You never know who will take you up on it. Pray for classroom volunteers who will make an impact with the students who need extra attention. God will hear your prayers!

DAY 17

Moses inspected the work and saw that they had done it just as the LORD had commanded. So Moses blessed them.

Exodus 39:43 NIV

B e prepared and avoid taking shortcuts to get the work done. Put in the time needed at the beginning of the year, and you will be blessed with the dividends of an organized and successful classroom for many years to come. Work on being as organized as possible. Talk to other teachers or your mentor to see what organizational system they use to keep track of what they are doing throughout the week. A good calendar will be your best friend. Record important information on the calendar such as meeting times and assignment due dates. One way to keep your life organized is through a cloud-based calendar. Google Calendar has many great features that will allow you to input work and personal schedules and then allow them to overlap if you want so you can see any potential conflicts. For your lessons and copies, it may be a good idea to have a set of hard copies around in case the computer server goes down.

If you do a good job organizing work this year, then next year will be easier to find lesson plans, copies, and any notes that you made to refine your craft. One suggestion for an organizational system is using a three-ring binder per unit in your content area(s). Place your scope and sequence in the front followed by the lesson plans then copies, etc. This allows you to access the unit lessons and assessments quickly, especially if you will be having a sub covering for you.

DAY 18

A generous person will prosper; whoever refreshes others will be refreshed.

PROVERBS 11:25 NIV

Try to avoid taking work home at the end of the day. This was a philosophy I learned during my first year of teaching. I had a great mentor teacher in my classroom so we were able to bounce ideas off each other during the day. One day I asked her, "How come you are always able to leave without taking work with you?" She said, "Life is too short to be spending all of my nights and weekends grading papers when I should be with my friends and family." I thought about that and realized she was right. I have too many things that I want to experience and relationships to cultivate rather than using that time to grade papers. You may want to consider coming in early to get paperwork done. There will be fewer distractions and lines for the copy machine anyway.

I frequently hear teachers talk about how many hours they are spending at school and long nights grading papers and spending time on the weekends in their classrooms. There are going to be times you have to grade papers, and there is no way around it. There are going to be deadlines that have to be met and assignments that need to be done. Working on the weekends and late at night should be the exception and not the rule. Take care of yourself, family, and friends. Doing this will give you energy and the patience to be a great teacher and sustain you throughout the entire year. Teaching is a tough profession and spending time with those that you care about will reenergize you for the work you are called to do.

DAY 19

"You should be a light for other people. Live so that they will see the good things you do and will praise your Father in heaven."

Matthew 5:16 NCV

G et systems in place in which students learn practices that make a classroom run smoother. These are more than just rules in the classroom; the procedures to having a student-led class will give more ownership to your students and taking some of the work off your plate. Do not assume your students know what your expectations are yet. It sounds silly, but even in middle school, students still struggle with how to behave in the hallway and in the restroom! Give fun demonstrations using students on how to practice appropriate behaviors in the various school environments. Students love to play the part of the naughty kid! All of these ways will help students understand the different expectations that are required of them in various locations throughout their school.

Part of the routine is knowing where everything is in your classroom; make sure during the first one or two days of class that you take a tour of your room, and that students know where to find everything. Demonstrate where the turn-in boxes are for their homework and how to submit assignments online. Get students signed up and registered for courses on the computer as needed. Get these housekeeping things out of the way so the ensuing months will be more productive and fun for both you and your students.

DAY 20: REFLECTION AND PRAYER

DAY 21

Finally, brothers and sisters, whatever is true, whatever is noble, whatever is right, whatever is pure, whatever is lovely, whatever is admirable—if anything is excellent or praiseworthy—think on such things.

Philippians 4:8 NIV

Keep the classroom management plan going. If students cannot follow the rules, and there will always be some, then provide a positive behavior incentive plan. It is not a bad idea to have a classroom positive behavior support plan for all students than a second tier plan for students who need additional interventions around behavior. Behaviors look different in all settings, so talk with your school psychologist or social worker about any students who you are concerned about. Some students may want your attention or attention from peers to avoid work, or because the task being asked of them may be too difficult. There are many other reasons, but these are just a few. Once you pinpoint a function of the behavior, then you know what the triggers are and about what time of day the actions occur.

The next step is developing a behavior plan for the student. This does not have to be a formal plan, but the student should be involved. Some students want to work for food or extra time with the teacher, but sometimes they just want free time to relax. For one student's reward, I let him bring his RC racing car to school because he had a great week! Mix it up and keep things fresh by allowing the students to pick the incentives. There are many great resources out there to help you with your behavior plans and motivations for student success.

DAY 22

*Therefore encourage one another and build
each other up, just as in fact you are doing.*

1 THESSALONIANS 5:11 NIV

S pend extra time on the "heavy hitters," those coming into the classroom with a past history which indicates you will need to work harder/smarter to reach them. Try and reach out to their previous teachers and parents to find their interests and any interventions that may have worked in the past. Try to establish positive behavior supports in your classroom. See what other teachers are doing across the grade level that will help provide consistency for students.

One way to help produce positive behavior in the classroom is the five-to-one approach. To promote positive action in the school, you should try and have a ratio of five praises to one redirection. Who does not like approval? Everyone needs a pick-me-up every now and again, and maybe your students do not get this at home. It makes us feel good to be recognized for something we did well. It makes us want to continue to keep doing our best. This is hard to do sometimes, and you definitely have to be intentional about it. This does not mean that you merely praise a student for getting out their pencil while they are working on an assignment. These praises need to be genuine and sincere, and that is when the student notices that you are looking for the good in them instead of the negative. Once they see that you are there to help them, hopefully, some or all of the negative behaviors will decline. Some students will need more intervention than this, but 5:1 is an excellent place to start for all students.

DAY 23

"Nevertheless, I will bring health and healing to it; I will heal my people and will let them enjoy abundant peace and security."

Jeremiah 33:6 NIV

Prepare to be sick. Then prepare a substitute teacher plan packet with procedures written down ahead of time. Have extra activities for a sub to do with your students. It never fails that around October, I always get sick! No matter how long I have taught, whether I have had the flu shot or not, I still get sick. No one likes to make lesson plans for a sub when they are already ill, especially at three or four in the morning. Have detailed lesson plans with routines and procedures for fire drills and tornado drills, and a list of students with medical needs.

Make sure you have a detailed emergency lesson plan that has extra copies in case you are too sick or have to run out of town before making lesson plans. If you are able to make your sub plans ahead of time, but cannot get to school, email your mentor or another grade level teacher, and they can help you out by printing materials and getting things set up for you. Remember to get the chocolate or a beverage of their choice for helping you. Make sure you are able to access the online substitute teacher system that your district has in place. The school office staff or other teachers may be able to provide you with a list of preferred substitutes who work well in your building. Put these numbers in your phone in case of an emergency or when you need that mental health day!

DAY 24

*You, LORD, give perfect peace to those who keep
their purpose firm and put their trust in you.*

ISAIAH 26:3 GNT

Homework should be manageable. There are different expectations of homework at each grade level. As a general rule, the elementary level has twenty minutes of reading every night. Usually, there is some other homework on top of that but no more than one hour per night. It gets a little harder at the middle school and high school levels with multiple classes all requiring outside work at some point. Make sure the practice is meaningful and not just busy work.

Families are busy, and I am sure you are too. Make sure that the homework assignments are manageable and critical to the content. Ask yourself if you are assessing their quality or quantity of the students' work. One thing is sure, all students could benefit from extra reading at home. Another reason to keep homework manageable is that they may require help from home with homework. If students did not grasp the concept in class, there is a good chance they will not be able to do it entirely on their own at home. You may have to make accommodations for students with their homework as needed.

DAY 25: REFLECTION AND PRAYER

DAY 26

"I was without clothes, and you gave me something to wear."
MATTHEW 25:36 NCV

Buy two to three extra Halloween costumes as you will find that a student will forget or cannot afford one. In elementary school, students enjoy wearing their Halloween costumes to school for their holiday party at the end of the day. Some students do not even come to school that day because they know they will not have a costume and do not want to feel embarrassed. I remember the day before Halloween a boy said he was not going to come the next day because he did not have a costume. I told him I would take care of it and the next day he was a ninja! He was grateful and pleased to just be a child who was having fun instead of worrying about his situation.

If you can, about a month before Halloween, start asking around to friends and families that may have old Halloween costumes that would fit students in your class. You will want to have a couple of various sizes for boys and girls. I let the students borrow them, but I also tell them that I will need them back for others to use in the future. I allowed them to keep them to use for trick or treating though. They usually bring me back some candy! Once Halloween is over, keep an eye out for costumes at a significant discount as stores are looking to stock their shelves for Thanksgiving. You will be a lifesaver for a kid who needs a costume.

DAY 27

Make a careful exploration of who you are and the work you have been given, and then sink yourself into that.

GALATIANS 6:4 THE MESSAGE

Teaching is more than just showing up every day at school and delivering the curriculum. Encourage and support your students for the activities they are participating in inside and outside of the classroom. Attend your students' activities when you can. This is another way to get to know your students outside of the classroom. Throughout the year, try to make it to one or two of these events. This helps to continue building relationships with your students, and also encourages them to pursue activities that they enjoy. It is always fun to talk with the students the next day about how well they did in their concert, plays, or sporting events.

I know a few teachers who coach sports or did activities such as Girls on the Run, which is a great activity that includes training and culminates with a 5k run/walk with all of the schools coming together to race. Events such as these are a great ways to show your support for students who have been training for months for their event. Some students may participate in Boy Scouts or Girl Scouts and may have an event such as the pinewood derby, etc., that they are really excited about, and would love for you to attend. Your students will remember all year that you came to their events, and it will make a lasting impact on their lives. When I was a student, I certainly remembered the teachers who came to my events.

DAY 28

Christ Jesus…made himself nothing by
taking the very nature of a servant…

PHILIPPIANS 2:5–7 NIV

S trive to be firm and consistent to set the tone, but at the same time, do not be afraid to change things if you find something is not working. Once you have your routines in place, you will find out what is working for your students and what might need to change. For example, make sure you change the seating chart once or twice during the first quarter to see who works well together and who cannot be near one another. Also, you may have to provide individual or class incentives for students being positive leaders in the classroom.

Good deed awards given to students for serving others in the school are celebrations that promote positive behavior in the classroom. Students can nominate one another from their own class and get a prize each week. During times with breaks coming up (Thanksgiving, Christmas, etc.), make these incentives more frequent to help students stay on track. Talk about examples of positive behavior, and continue to revisit the expectations and the social contract you drafted at the beginning of the year. Keep trying to reward those who are doing the right thing each day. It is easy to reward the student who always acts up for being good one time. There is definitely a place for that type of incentive plan, but also do not forget about the students who put in the hard work day in and day out to help make your class run smoothly.

DAY 29

Accept one another, then, just as Christ accepted you, in order to bring praise to God.

ROMANS 15:7 NIV

Know the town/city where your students live. I have never lived in the same town or city where I taught. Even if you do not live in the same town as your students, take some to see the area. During this time, see where students shop, recreate, and other sights and scenery in the area. Throughout the school year, your students will talk to you about things that they do in the city where they live. Having some background knowledge of these areas will enable you to relate better with your students.

I always shopped at the local grocery store for student treats and snacks in the mornings before school started. Sometimes you see students there, and it is fun to see them outside of the school. Be careful what you put in your shopping cart though! Hopefully, parents understand that you are an adult and have a life outside of school, but it is just as easy to shop somewhere else for those items.

DAY 30: REFLECTION AND PRAYER

DAY 31

For this reason, since the day we heard about you, we have not stopped praying for you. We continually ask God to fill you with the knowledge of his will through all the wisdom and understanding that the Spirit gives.

Colossians 1:9 NIV

D o not be afraid to ask for help. There will be times during the first few weeks of school when you will be overwhelmed with different tasks such as grading, new teacher orientation, etc. It is a sign of strength to ask for help. Check in with your mentor or other teachers in your department or grade level. They can help you prioritize things that will need to be completed soon and what can wait until the end of the week or later. Next year, you will be able to juggle all of these tasks, but this year, it is vital to get some direction. If you are a special education teacher, you will also need to start looking at upcoming IEP meetings and reevaluations. Start to plan your calendar now and work with a coworker to plan your IEP schedule for the year.

The other teachers in the school want to help you because we have all been there before. They know what it is like to be new and to have to learn everything all at once. We wish we were drinking out of a fountain, but sometimes the information is like drinking from a firehose! Be humble and gracious enough to ask for help early and often throughout the year. This will only help you and your students grow together in your first year.

DAY 32

*"Ask, and God will give to you. Search, and you
will find. Knock, and the door will open for you."*

MATTHEW 7:7 NIV

Ask some of your colleagues or research how others organize their lesson plans. There are so many time-saving ideas. You may want to utilize a lesson plan book software (Planbook, etc.). There are some pretty great tools out there for keeping track of your lesson plans. Teachers in my current district have to submit weekly lesson plans digitally so our administrators can see them if they choose to read them. My grade level teams meet once a week to go over lesson plans and formulate the learning targets and success criteria for each lesson. Let the software do some of this work for you. This way you can focus more time on what is really important, which is differentiating your lessons to meet the needs of your students.

Planbook and other software help teachers load their lessons and input standards for each lesson and content area without teachers having to go back and look them up in their curriculum guide. The significance of this software is that I can transfer my plans to a new school year or easily copy/paste them where they fit. The program automatically archives your lessons for you. These programs are one way in which you can work smarter instead of harder.

DAY 33

Bless the LORD...who forgives all your iniquities...

PSALM 103: 2–3 NKJV

A new teacher needs to understand that lesson plans will fail. I have had this happen to me more times than I can count. One time, I had this excellent lesson plan with videos and other links to an independent WebQuest research project for students that I worked on for hours. On the day that we were to work on the project, which also happened to be a day that my principal stopped in to observe me, the internet connection was lost, and the server was down. Everything I had worked on was inaccessible, and I had twenty-five students plus my principal all looking at me for direction.

What did I do next? I just laughed and apologized to my students. I talked to them about how sometimes things do not go the way you planned and being flexible is important. Luckily, I had the next day's copies and lesson ready, so we ended up flipping the lessons around. It is definitely an uncomfortable feeling when you fall very short in front of the students you are teaching. It is more important to model to your students that you are human too, and that you learn from your mistakes. Hopefully, they will follow in your footsteps.

DAY 34

"So do not fear, for I am with you; do not be dismayed, for I am your God. I will strengthen you and help you; I will uphold you with my righteous right hand."

Isaiah 41:10 NIV

Pray for guidance and for your students. I found this to be extremely helpful as I often work with students with behavior issues and poor home lives who tend to struggle more in school. Some mornings are just chaotic with getting our kids around trying to get ready for work, rush to school, and have twenty-five to twenty-eight students who need us to be on our game every day. If you take the time to pray and to follow His will in your life, you have all of the support you need to get through some of those tough days.

Pray for strength, energy, and wisdom as you list students by name with whom you would like to make a difference. Even if you are not a Christian, just thinking about your students and how you can positively affect their lives will significantly impact your mindset and help you to have a better day. This job is hard, and we cannot do it alone. There are definitely days when we do not feel like going into work because of our own problems and situations. May the Lord give you strength, wisdom, and patience for you to provide your best to all students and staff that you will encounter today.

DAY 35: REFLECTION AND PRAYER

_____

_____

_____

_____

_____

_____

_____

_____

_____

_____

_____

_____

_____

_____

_____

_____

_____

_____

_____

_____

_____

_____

DAY 36

All Scripture is God-breathed and is useful for teaching, rebuking, correcting and training in righteousness, so that the servant of God may be thoroughly equipped for every good work.

2 Timothy 3:16–17 NIV

Have a conduct management plan in place (preferably one that does not use bribery!). Since this is your first or second year of teaching, talk with some veteran teachers about management structures they have in place. Ask them what has worked well and what has not worked so well. You want to reward positive behavior, but students should know that the expectation is to be an active participant in the classroom.

Sometimes visuals are helpful or a quiet conversation with a students to help them be redirected. Ensure that you are consistent when they have not followed the expectations. Talk to them about appropriate behaviors and what happens if they cannot act appropriately in the classroom. Some students like to be removed from the classroom because they will be avoiding more work. You will need to know the students well to tweak your system for some situations. Overall though, you should have a plan in place that you can easily communicate with your students as well as enforce. Do not tell a student that they will have to stay after school until their work is done, but in reality, you have to leave right away to a dentist appointment. Make sure parents are aware of your management system as well. This will help keep lines of communication open if there is a problem in the classroom.

DAY 37

Who is wise and understanding among you? Let them show it by their good life, by deeds done in the humility that comes from wisdom.

James 3:13 NIV

B ecome friends with the custodians and lunch staff. These folks, along with the secretaries, run the school. These are the people who can help you out in a pinch, especially if you have a sick student, need something fixed or removed from the classroom, or can be a listening ear to a student in your class. You never know the impact that a lunchroom worker or a custodian will have on your students.

When I was teaching middle school, our custodian had a fish tank inside his office. I had one student with some emotional needs and the only person in the school he would talk to in a time of crisis would be our custodian. He would walk around with the student, and that student would help him on a couple of projects for about five to ten minutes, feed the fish, grab a piece of candy, and head back to class ready to go. The custodian did not get paid extra to work with our student, but he took the time to help a student in need.

I cannot tell you how many times I have seen lunch workers and custodians go above and beyond their position to help others. Help them out when you get a chance, and get to know them on a personal level. Ask them about their own families and what they are up to outside of work. Write down their birthday on your calendar and send them a card saying thank you for all they do for you and your school!

DAY 38

I pray that the eyes of your heart may be enlightened in order that you may know the hope to which he has called you, the riches of his glorious inheritance in his holy people.

EPHESIANS 1:18 NIV

This year is going to be pretty busy and often chaotic at times. As school gets underway, make a list of what your priorities are both professionally and socially. Set some goals that you would like to achieve. It is easy to get so caught up in the day to day business that we forget about the big picture and as soon as you know it, the year will have gone by!

Many people make New Year's resolutions in January. I try to make them for the school year as well. I take a look at all of the essential things in my life such as family, school, friends, church, hobbies, etc. Rank these from the highest priority to the lowest. Your teaching and work outside of the classroom will build a good foundation for your career that first year, but it should not be the only part of your life. Try and find some balance. If you are finding that school work and grading are creeping more into other areas of your life, take a step back and see if you need to readjust what you are doing. There will definitely be times of the year that are busy for you such as during conferences, report cards, etc., but try to find a way to hit all of your personal and professional goals and you will have a memorable school year!

DAY 39

Be anxious for nothing, but in everything by prayer and supplication, with thanksgiving, let your requests be made known to God; and the peace of God, which surpasses all understanding, will guard your hearts and minds through Christ Jesus.

PHILIPPIANS 4:6–7 NKJV

Try not to worry about things that are out of your control. One thing you cannot control is the environment in which students come from each day. You cannot control how parents treat their children. You also cannot control who comes to your door at the beginning of the year either. You can control how you respond to others in various situations. There are 185 days in which you have an opportunity to change things that are within your control.

You do have control over providing a safe environment during the school day, and providing these children with a chance at high-quality instruction. You also have the opportunity to model behavior that is kind, fair, and just for all of your students. The structure you provide in the classroom will benefit the students in the future. Try and pick out a student in your class that needs extra attention and kindness. Take them under your wing and give them opportunities to shine where they might not at home. Students may just find their calling with your guidance.

DAY 40: REFLECTION AND PRAYER

DAY 41

For we are God's handiwork, created in Christ Jesus to do good works, which God prepared in advance for us to do.

Ephesians 2:10 NIV

Teach your students, not the curriculum. There is a delicate balance between getting through the state standards and knowing where your students are throughout the year. Benchmark pre-assessments in reading, writing, and math will be important indicators of your students' knowledge or any gaps they may have that need to be addressed. Sometimes you have to go slow to go fast throughout the year. Just like setting a foundation for your social contract and behavior, the same applies to all the content areas. You have to build foundation skills, background knowledge, and an understanding of expectations related to the content to be successful for the rest of the year.

One way to help set your students up for success is to have them set goals. We often have students set up a student success binder. This includes goal tracking sheets for reading, writing, and math. No matter what the grade level, they can set goals in these areas. Students are well aware of what their strengths and needs are in each content area. Periodically revisiting the students' goals with them will help to identify any areas of concern, and also show their progress throughout the school year. These are also great tools for conferences in the fall and spring to show growth. Make sure to find a way to celebrate this growth with your students.

DAY 42

The unfolding of your words gives light;
it gives understanding to the simple.

PSALM 119:130 NIV

Make meaningful conversations with students. I often have students come into my room for lunch or come and hang out in the morning before school starts. Usually, during these times, I am also working on completing paperwork, grading, and setting up the classroom for the day.

Students want to talk with teachers for a variety of reasons. They want to share some exciting things from the weekend, tragedies in their family, or problems they are having with their friends. They trust you enough to come to you with the good things and troubles that they are going through. Try to model active listening skills. Take the time to listen to them even if you will not get your work done. They will appreciate it and see you as a trusting adult who cares for them. If you must get your email or lesson plan typed up, kindly ask the student to wait a minute or so until you finish what you are doing so you can give your full attention to that student.

DAY 43

"Every day, hundreds of thousands of new parents bring home babies that they have no idea how to care for, and despite that, mankind has persisted for years. The same thing for teaching. You're going to do fine and when you make the guaranteed goofs, it's not the end of the world."

—Kevin Miller, Middle School Resource Teacher

New teachers need to know that they are going to make mistakes and that it is alright. One mistake I made was giving a test on the Friday before a holiday (scores plummeted). Also, I was so concerned about the curriculum and getting through all of my content that I hardly took quality time to get to know my students that first year.

Mistakes allow you to identify your strengths and where your areas of focus need to be the during the following school year. If you are lucky enough to be in the same building teaching the same subject area, you will have a better grasp of the curriculum than the previous year, so you can focus more on how you are delivering that to your students. Maybe you are standing and lecturing a lot this year and want to change to more of a student-led collaborative model for next year. Make sure you are comfortable before you make significant changes. It is better to make a few small changes and have them affect student achievement in a positive way than make many changes and not see any improvement.

DAY 44

I urge, then, first of all, that petitions, prayers, intercession and thanksgiving be made for all people—for kings and all those in authority, that we may live peaceful and quiet lives in all godliness and holiness.

1 Timothy 2:1–2 NIV

Pray. Praying for students and their families is paramount. The old saying that it takes a village to raise a child is so true. Families in your classrooms will have various dynamics and issues come up throughout the school year. Spend time in prayer for families of your students who are going through seasons of hardships. Students may lose a family member or friends during a school year. Your support and prayer will be a firm foundation to stand on.

Pray for specific students and their families. Reach out to the families in your room and ask if they need anything. Pray for that family and help to provide resources for them to get through their difficult times. Pray that during conversations throughout the day, you are speaking life to your students and building them up rather than looking to criticize. It takes a village and prayer to raise children because we cannot do it alone.

DAY 45: REFLECTION AND PRAYER

Second Quarter

(OCTOBER-JANUARY)

DAY 46

Put on the apron of humility, to serve one another...

1 PETER 5:5 GNT

Give parents options for conferences. In October and November many things are going on for families with conferences being one of them. If you want a good turnout at parent/teacher conferences, especially at the middle school and high school level, try and give as many options as possible for parents to participate. Some parents may not be able to attend the actual conference but may be able to go over a portfolio with their student and return it showing that they had a conversation with their child. Then later you can follow up with a phone call or email. Some families have multiple conferences they have to attend in the fall or in the spring, so sending out your schedule will help families to coordinate their schedules so they are able to attend conferences.

At the elementary school level, you may have one or two days to get twenty-eight to thirty conferences completed. This is hardly enough time, especially when you only have about fifteen minutes per parent to discuss strengths and concerns. Offer some other times for parents to meet such as before school, during lunch, or during the week of conferences. Parents will appreciate your flexibility, and you will be able to have some breathing room to have a more productive discussion with parents.

DAY 47

"Love your neighbor as yourself."

GALATIANS 5:14 NIV

For a new teacher to be successful in their first semester, they need to be very flexible and open to learning. This probably goes for veteran teachers as well. There are going to be some days when a lot of unexpected things come your way. Emergency drills, student absences, etc. are going to are going to have an effect on your plans. Be open and flexible to adjust as you need to. The work will get done so stay the course. Make sure you keep the big picture in mind for why you are there.

Help other staff members in your building. There will be times when a colleague has to go to a doctor appointment, or there is an emergency with one of their children. If you are able, step in and supervise their class for a little while. This often happens because of substitute cancellations. One time we had a substitute teacher cancel and the replacement substitute did not show up either! Sometimes you just get through the day the best way you can and help out your colleagues along the way. They will likely pay it forward for you down the road when you might need it.

DAY 48

When you talk, do not say harmful things, but say what people need—words that will help others become stronger.

EPHESIANS 4:29 NCV

P repare for parent-teacher conferences. Bring a lot of water because you will be talking a lot! Ask parents to give you insight on their child (do not do all the talking). Make sure parents leave with more information then when they came, and a sense that you know and care about their child. At the elementary level, parents and teachers usually talk for about fifteen minutes, and then the next group comes in. Often at the middle and high school levels, you are in a larger setting, and there might be long lines of people waiting to talk with you about their student. One way to help make this process smoother is to come up with a one-page report discussing how their student is doing overall with academics, work habits, and social interactions.

If the parents can have something to take home and look over, then you can focus on more meaningful conversations and pressing issues that you or the parents want to address during the conference. This document could include some benchmark and progress monitoring scores for your content area(s) as well as some areas of strength and improvement. Talk to the parents about goals and what they want for their child by the end of the year. Offer to meet at an additional time if needed, since your time will be limited during conferences.

DAY 49

*Do not let any unwholesome talk come out of your mouths,
but only what is helpful for building others up according to
their needs, that it may benefit those who listen.*

EPHESIANS 4:29 NIV

When talking to parents via email, phone, or in person during an IEP or conferences, start with student strengths then then address concerns. Oftentimes, when parents answer the phone and their child's teacher is on the other end, they may become defensive. This may not be the first time they have heard from the school for the wrong reasons.

One way to help parents let their guard down and to open the conversation is to start off by describing what you appreciate about their child, and the attributes they bring to the classroom. I once had a student who had poor attendance, never did work in class, and was consistently a disruption to others. When I talked to the parent, I started by saying that Johnny was always prepared for class and that I appreciated it. I did leave out the fact that he only brought mechanical pencils without lead each day. The point is you can find something positive in every student that you can share with them and their parents.

DAY 50: REFLECTION AND PRAYER

DAY 51

Whatever work you do, do your best.

ECCLESIASTES 9:10 NCV

Practice your procedures with your students until they understand what you mean. Then practice them EVERY time the students are not meeting the expectation that you or they have set. School expectations look different in the hallways, bathrooms, lunchroom, gym, and the classroom. Take the time to go through the different environments in the school, and describe why the expectations are different in each setting. Practice even the smallest expectations daily in your classroom throughout the year.

If you want students to turn in papers in a semi-orderly fashion, then practice what you want to see. If they do it, but not exactly how you want it done, try it again. I told the students early in the year at every grade level I taught at when they left our room, it had to look as neat as when they came in. As you can imagine with anywhere between twenty and thirty kids in the room, it could get pretty messy. Before we went anywhere, the expectation was that the room was picked up. After many rounds of practice, students started taking care of their supplies while they were working and saw that this was much easier than saving it all up for the end of class.

DAY 52

"Teaching is, in my mind, the noblest of professions. So much goes into preparation for it, a preparation that never stops. And training young minds to be the citizens of tomorrow is giving society a gift that not many can give."

—LARRY CARTER, RETIRED FIFTH-GRADE TEACHER

Try to see the big picture of your units and what you want your students to achieve. In the beginning, it is tough to find time to look ahead, so if you can do that, it makes planning more manageable. Now that you have some breathing room (hopefully), look ahead at the units and make sure you are on track to finish at the right time. Talk with your colleagues to see what critical standards you need to teach. Hopefully, a pre-assessment, will give you an indication of what your students need during the unit. If they already know the material, then you can move on to the next standard.

If possible, try to combine your units across content areas. If you can tie in Newton's laws with your current math lesson, for example, you can be more efficient with your lesson planning, and it makes more connections for your students. These connections, and real-life experiences across the curriculum, will help them retain the information better because you are looking at it from a variety of lenses such as math, science, writing, etc. You could even talk with your PE teacher about using Newton's laws in their class! This is hard to do with every single lesson every day, but maybe an overall culminating project is the first place to start for cross-curricular work.

DAY 53

And whatever you do, whether in word or deed, do it all in the name of the Lord Jesus, giving thanks to God the Father through him.

COLOSSIANS 3:17 NIV

The honeymoon period is probably over by now. Some students might be acting out and are doing so in a variety of ways. Seek advice and information from the social worker/mentor/parent and student about the reason for the behaviors. These professionals in your building have years of experience with the student's challenges that you may be currently facing. They may not have the answer right away for you and your particular situation, but they are able to use their own resources to help you guide your student back in the right direction.

There may be times especially in upper elementary and the secondary level that a student's medication(s) are being readjusted for one reason or another. Keep open communication with the parents as well because they may be seeing some of the same behaviors or worse at home and wondering if they are acting this way at school. Coming together and meeting with the student can also be beneficial. This shows the students that you are working with their parents closely to help them achieve their potential. In most cases, you will build a stronger relationship with families. You will also gain some great resources and knowledge from your colleagues, but most importantly, help the student get back on track.

DAY 54

Sanctify them by the truth; your word is truth.

JOHN 17:17 NIV

D o not ever engage in a power struggle with a student. Ever. You know your students well and what you are seeing day to day is pretty consistent with what you will see throughout the year. Some students may begin to test your limits if they have not done so already. This is normal. The students are trying to see what will be allowed and not allowed in the classroom. Remind the students of the social contract that has been established, and follow through with your expectations.

The times that students are talking back or engaging in a power struggle with you will never benefit you even if you win. Tell the student what you want them to do and what will happen when they are not doing what you ask. Do not use a lot of words, especially when students are escalated. Students at that level are not ready for a conversation, so they may need to calm down outside of the classroom. If they are willing to calm down and ready to process, invite them to come back to class. Always work to preserve the relationship between the student and the teacher while at the same time holding the student accountable for the learning in your classroom.

DAY 55: REFLECTION AND PRAYER

DAY 56

*"Don't be afraid to let the students see who you are.
It will help to create mutual respect."*

—SUSAN WILKINS, ADJUNCT PROFESSOR, CALVIN UNIVERSITY

Be equitable. Try hard not to show favoritism—students know. This can be hard sometimes because some students are always doing the right thing, turning in homework, and consistently following the expectations in your classroom. These students are your go-to kids if you need something. Do not call on them every time or ask them to do every job for you. Likewise, you do not want to spend all of your time with students who have behavior issues, etc. This is a fine line to walk, but you need to be dedicated to it otherwise you may go from one side to the other.

There definitely will be times when you have to help students through situations that they are going through, and give them extra attention. Remember there are other students in your class as well that are looking for that same attention even though they may not voice their opinion or express what is going on outside of school. Depending on the grade level you work with, try and spend some extra time in conversation with each student over a two-week period. Talk about topics unrelated to school, so the students know that you are interested in them, and not just if they are getting the content. This may be more challenging at the secondary level, but make it a goal to talk with a certain number of students, and you will more likely reach out to more students than if you did not set a goal for yourself.

DAY 57

And this is my prayer: that your love may abound more and more in knowledge and depth of insight, so that you may be able to discern what is best and may be pure and blameless for the day of Christ...

PHILIPPIANS 1:9–10 NIV

Be a keen observer of your students and write down anecdotal notes. Think about the students in the class who get along with others and those who do not get along. Think of a way to create a seating chart that allows for collaborative work along with building a sense of community. Some students act differently outside of the classroom. Some students may be reserved in class, but they are very animated and competitive in PE. I once had a selectively mute student in my class. She would never talk to adults or other kids at school. One day, I contacted her mother regarding an upcoming field trip, and who did I hear yelling in the background? My student! She was acting like a regular kid at home, but acted differently at school. I would not have known that if I had not called her home that day.

If you have not done so already, spend some time with your students observing how they interact with others outside of your classroom. You may be able to link up some students if you see that at recess and lunch they are having a tough time finding others to play or sit with. Students need to be comfortable in your classroom as well as in the different environments of the school.

DAY 58

For I was hungry and you gave me food, I was thirsty and you gave me drink, I was a stranger and you welcomed me.

MATTHEW 25:35 ESV

Have breakfast food in your room. Take a survey of what your students eat for breakfast. If basic needs like food are not met, then students might exhibit undesirable behaviors throughout the day. I always have various breakfast snacks such as cereal bars, granola bars, etc., in my desk for students who may need a little something extra.

There might be students who depend on you daily for that breakfast snack. Many of your students may qualify for free/reduced lunch and breakfast at school. If the student often comes late to school and misses a meal, arrange to have breakfast eaten inside the classroom during the first half hour of the day. Places like Sam's Club, Costco, etc., sell breakfast snack items in bulk so you can stock up. There might also be some grant money you can use for this purpose as well. The food bank also may donate food if they know you are giving it to qualifying students. This is another way to build healthy kids and a healthy rapport with them. They will know you are looking out for their best interests.

DAY 59

*And let us not grow weary of doing good, for
in due season we will reap, if we do not give up.*

GALATIANS 6:9 ESV

Now that you know your students, rules and routines have been established, and your classroom is organized to your liking, start analyzing data. How are your students doing? Try to determine which students need more support and enrichment. Are there students who are presenting behaviors that are impeding their ability to make progress? Ask your mentor, instructional support advisor, and administrators to help you find supplemental activities or behavioral tools that will address the identified needs. There are some great programs out there to help with enrichment and remediation. Many students will be able to use a program independently, but many will need hands-on support.

Ask for a volunteer to help in the classroom to help you when you are providing interventions and/or enrichment activities. Remediation has shown to be most effective when in a small group setting. The students are more willing to participate, and individual needs can be addressed when there are fewer distractions. The volunteer could help you with your small groups or help to troubleshoot questions that the rest of the class has while you are supporting small groups of students. That extra set of hands will be invaluable. The students will also appreciate getting to know another adult in the room as well.

DAY 60: REFLECTION AND PRAYER

DAY 61

May the grace of the Lord Jesus Christ, and the love of God,
and the fellowship of the Holy Spirit be with you all.

2 CORINTHIANS 13:14 NIV

I never bought the admonition that teachers should not be friends with their students. Once you have established that you are the teacher, that you deserve their respect, that your word is ultimately the word going forward, then friendship is the best possible thing to happen! I enjoy being with my friends more than anything else—why should a teacher be exempt from that? Being a friend means being there when times are great and when things are going lousy for you and your students. You will be able to laugh and enjoy each other, but also help each other grieve when there are hard times.

Another attribute of a good friend is keeping each other accountable. Your role as a teacher is to help teach responsibility, honesty, and integrity to your students. This is not always easy, but a good friend will always try to help, encourage, and hold the other accountable because it is the right thing to do. All friends may go through some tough times, but being willing to help will make your relationship stronger with your students.

DAY 62

So do not throw away your confidence; it will be richly rewarded. You need to persevere so that when you have done the will of God, you will receive what he has promised.

HEBREWS 10:35–36 NIV

Keep the classroom management plan going. Begin to support those struggling with academics with lunch help, after-school help, or support at home for parents. Bring concerns to others in a child study or team setting to get additional support. The second and third quarters of the school year are vital for closing the achievement gap for concepts lost over the summer, and learning new information that are at grade level standards. Use this time efficiently and let the data drive your instruction.

If you are seeing that students are starting to fall behind, try to pinpoint what is going on. For example, if a student consistently is getting word problems wrong in math, there is a chance that their reading may need some support as well. More math problems may not solve the issue, but an intervention of reading support could help the student to use strategies for comprehending and solving math problems. A few helpful people to help to identify Tier 2 interventions in the classroom are the school psychologist or special education staff. Start with one intervention for the student(s) and track the results for a few weeks to see if there is a change. If not, another intervention might be needed. This is definitely the time of year to start adding those interventions into daily and weekly practice.

DAY 63

The Lord is not slow in keeping his promise, as some understand slowness. Instead he is patient with you, not wanting anyone to perish, but everyone to come to repentance.

2 PETER 3:9 NIV

Expect escalated behaviors from some students with emotional or socio-economic needs. This is true for all longer breaks in the school year, such as Christmas, spring break, and definitely around summer vacation. The behaviors can look differently for the students in your class. You might have some students who act out verbally or physically. There may be students who are absent more absent more leading up to a break, do not engage with peers, or do not complete classwork as they have done in the past. Many students struggle during unstructured times such as passing periods in the hallways, recess, and in the lunchroom.

Since you know to expect these behaviors in the coming days or weeks before a break, you might be able to prepare your students more for them and help them to be more successful. Many children do not have a lot of interaction during extended breaks from school because their parents are working, so they are left on their own all day. Try to spend some extra time each day with these students leading up to break, and continue to let them know that you care, and that you want them to finish strong. You could also create some kind of behavior contract with the student before a break. If the does a great job class, then the student gets a reward that is agreed upon by both parties. It is a way for both you and the student to start the break on a positive note.

DAY 64

*Let us not become weary in doing good, for at a proper time
we will reap a harvest if we do not give up.*

GALATIANS 6:9 NIV

Now that you have established patterns in the classroom, stick with them! If they are not working, make modifications, but do not abandon your efforts to have a student-centered classroom. You should not be doing the work that self-managing students should be doing. These efforts will pay off as you continue to develop into a facilitator of curriculum and instruction. Revisit and keep students accountable for turning in their work. Have students correct their work and make corrections on assignments. It seems like the student will get more out of the revisions when they can see what they missed themselves rather than the teacher just marking it wrong.

Teach students how to check their own grades and see if they have missing assignments. In middle school and high school, this should be an expectation, and for the younger grades, they will need some instruction on how to do this. Spend time with these procedures and working with your different programs so students can be more self-sufficient. Place materials they will need daily in their workspace so they can quickly get to them when needed. This could be done with a small basket, shelf, etc. This will help to eliminate minutes on a transition during instructional time.

DAY 65: REFLECTION AND PRAYER

DAY 66

So, whether you eat or drink, or whatever
you do, do all to the glory of God.

1 CORINTHIANS 10:31 ESV

Take a student out to lunch every now and then. This may seem like a small thing, but students really appreciate it! You could have lunch with a student for a variety of reasons. Maybe they set a goal for academics and they got a high score on their test, or met their goal for reading minutes for the month. I often have lunch with students who struggle with behaviors and academics in school. Part of the behavior agreement that we agree on is a reward for lunch at the end of the month if they meet their behavioral and work completion goals each week.

Food can be a huge motivator for students, especially a special treat. Some students I have had in the past really liked Chinese food, so it was a special day for them when we would eat Chinese together and talk about how great they did on their goals, and how their perseverance has paid off. This is also a good way to get to know the student better. Great conversations and food go hand in hand. That is why many business deals occur around a lunch or dinner! Breaking bread together helps to feed the body and the soul. Try having lunch with a few students this month and see what positive changes happen in your classroom.

DAY 67

*Each of us should please our neighbors
for their good, to build them up.*

ROMANS 15:2 NIV

Try giving an extra recess or other incentives for compliments made to classmates from peers. This is a great reward for students, but it also promotes awareness to treat each other with mutual respect. For the upper grades, maybe it is giving the students some extra time to listen to music, play games, etc. If you teach multiple classes or sections, you could even make it a competition to promote positive behavior in the classroom and around the school. Let the students decide on the incentive, but make sure you model what the compliment or good deed could and should look like.

The beginning and middle of the year is a great time to practice and relearn expectations while on the school's campus. The compliments or good deeds, whatever you decide, need to be sincere. Model positive behavior have students come up with examples of what this behavior should look like in the classroom. If it comes from the students, you will have better buy-in, which produces better results. You want all of your students to be respectful and considerate of others when they are older, and this is one avenue that you could use to teach this skill. You would be rewarding them for intentionally helping others.

DAY 68

I work and struggle, using Christ's great strength that works so powerfully in me.

COLOSSIANS 1:29 NCV

Some days you will run out of plans before you run out of the day. For example, the school schedule will change and you no longer have a prep period. Do not get backed into a wall. Always have a backup plan for those days when you need to teach an extra lesson, so it is a productive activity and not just a time-filler. The time that you have is precious, and all students have skills that could be enriched or remediated.

There are some great resources out there for these types of activities. If you have enough technology for students to work individually or in pairs, they could go onto some online websites based on the unit you are teaching at the current time. My students recently finished a web quest on themes or morals from stories. This project covers a multitude of standards which include twenty-first-century technology skills. The students are able to navigate through literature, videos, and organizers to help answer questions based on the research they have compiled over the previous two days. The students seem to enjoy it because they are jumping into the learning instead of having the teacher just lecturing to them. Give the students the tools and let them go! You will be surprised how much more them get out of your lesson when you are a facilitator rather than a lecturer.

DAY 69

May our Lord Jesus Christ himself and God our Father encourage you and strengthen you in every good thing you do and say.

2 THESSALONIANS 2:17 NCV

You will start to wonder why you ever decided to be a teacher in the first place. This is totally normal. Every teacher has this feeling in the first couple years of teaching. One time I calculated how much I got paid hourly, and it was very depressing. Students will test your limits, sometimes daily, and there is always work to be done. Sometimes, it sounds so much better to have a job where you punch in and punch out and leave everything at the door. There is a reason you are on this journey. You give selflessly and do not expect anything in return. You care!

When things seem to be going south, remember why you chose this profession in the first place and about the lives you have already enriched. I am sure you can think back to student teaching and recall how your experience affected students in a positive way, such as, when teaching a lesson, playing a game, or being a shoulder to cry on. This profession is not easy, and you have to be ready to give 110% every day because these kids deserve it. Now that I am a parent, I have a whole new perspective on teaching. Each student who walks through that door is someone's pride and joy. We would do anything for our own kids, and we must do the same for our students. Stay the course and try to find some time to refresh and relax!

DAY 70: REFLECTION AND PRAYER

DAY 71

*When pride comes, then comes disgrace,
but with humility comes wisdom.*

PROVERBS 11:2 NIV

As you teach, you learn what works and what does not work in your classroom. Sometimes it may take some trial and error. Keep pushing through, and know that you are making an incredible difference in the lives of so many students! I always told my students during the first year, "I apologize in advance if this lesson does not work out. It's my first time trying it, so we will learn and grow together." This gives you the freedom to make mistakes and the students know that you are trying your best for them. They do not want the same old curriculum from the book every day, so mixing it up for them and trying something new keeps it fresh and interesting.

You will know pretty quickly what type of management style works for you. Some teachers give "the look," and everyone knows that they mean business. I was never that good at providing a look unless I really needed it. Find a management system that works for you because trying to force yourself into a system that you do not honestly believe in will cause much more stress. Find a colleague in your school that you can bounce some ideas off of to see how you can improve your management system. Your students are forgiving, and if you admit when things are not going well, then they will be on board to try something new.

DAY 72

Do nothing out of selfish ambition or vain conceit. Rather, in humility value others above yourselves, not looking to your own interests but each of you to the interests of the others.

PHILIPPIANS 2:3–4 NIV

What you say to your colleagues, families, and others using school email is part of public record and could be used at any time if requested. Our administrator's words have always stuck with me. She said, "Remember that whatever you say is out there and could be on the front page of the newspaper." This does not mean that you should not bring up topics to parents that you are concerned about because you are worried that they will sue you at some point. If you do have parents with a tough student, it would be a wise idea to seek counsel from your administrator on how to communicate with this family.

One way to address issues that you are concerned about is to arrange a meeting with the parents with an administrator or another teacher present. A general rule of thumb, if you need to have a crucial conversation with someone, do not do it over email. This just leads to drawn out conversations and words taken out of context. It is hard to know if someone is being sarcastic over email as well. Wait for twenty-four hours to reply to harsh emails. Ask God for clarity and to choose the right words for the situation.

DAY 73

Honor the LORD with your wealth,
with the first fruits of all your crops...

Proverbs 3:9 NIV

Now that things are starting to settle down a little, check your finances. If this is your first job, you are not getting paid a lot, but more than in college. Seek advice to help handle your money. Set up a retirement account. Your district may match your contributions. The money that you set aside will compound in interest annually. Talk with a financial advisor about the amount of money you would be making if you invested now rather than waiting until later in your career.

The best way to set this up is to have it taken from your paycheck as a direct deposit. I have tried it the other way where you have to be diligent about making contributions to your retirement account. When it came down to it, I was not as disciplined as I needed to be and something always came up that I needed to pay for or wanted to buy. This way it is kind of like out of sight, out of mind. You will be happy down the road when you have a great jump start on your retirement. It will automatically go into your account, and they will send you statements quarterly so you can see if your investments are working well for you, or if you need to make changes. Seek wise counsel with your money and let your money work for you!

DAY 74

As water reflects the face, so one's life reflects the heart.

PROVERBS 27:19 NIV

Y ou ARE a role model. You should not be a teacher if you cannot handle that mantle. Yes, you were hired to teach students skills and strategies to further their education, but if you do not model those skills and strategies presented with honesty, integrity, and kindness, you are not a teacher. Your life well-lived should be an extension of your teaching. Many students do not have a consistent person at home who will help them stay the course and make the right choices. Every student needs you!

Your students are watching your every move and taking note. They notice how you talk with colleagues, and with students when they are having a bad day. Teach your students about grace, forgiveness, being honest, and keeping their word. Love one another as you love yourself. Let your students know when you have made a mistake. Your students will respect you for it. Assure them that no matter what, you will always care for them in your classroom. The Golden Rule is one to live by each day, and living it out in your classroom will pave the way for your students to follow your lead.

DAY 75: REFLECTION AND PRAYER

DAY 76

"Leave all the afternoon for exercise and recreation, which are as necessary as reading. I will rather say more necessary because health is worth more than learning."

—THOMAS JEFFERSON

The days are getting shorter, but that is a perfect time to start a hobby. A teacher is a huge part of who you are, but it should not define who you are as a person. When the weather turns cooler, and the days become shorter, get involved in something you have always wanted to do. Set a goal that you will start a new hobby, or get back into one that you have put off for a while. It will refresh your mind and body!

Try to get more involved with your church as well. I remember when I first started teaching it felt like the job was consuming my entire life. Hopefully, things are slowing down a little, and you can start or continue to build relationships within your church. Maybe you had to move away to begin your new teaching position, and you are searching for a home church. Make sure you take some time to visit and pray about each church you attend. Find one that will help you develop into the person you want to become. No matter the hobby or volunteer activity you choose, it will help you recharge and refocus the priorities in your life.

DAY 77

Each one must give as he has decided in his heart, not reluctantly or under compulsion, for God loves a cheerful giver.

2 CORINTHIANS 9:7 ESV

Get in touch with families to see if they need support during the Christmas season. Sometimes they will take you up on it. There are programs out there to assist families in need. This time of year can be one of high anxiety and worry for both kids and their parents. There may be families you know of that are worried about providing basic needs for their family.

Ask your administrator or social worker about possible programs in your school that will assist families in need with food, clothing, and Christmas presents. In many cases, schools will partner with local agencies to help donate and deliver food, clothing, and gifts to families in need over the holidays. If you can be part of these programs, it is an excellent opportunity to show God's love for people in their time of need. Many of these families will not ask for help, so please reach out to them to see if they might need something. After the holidays are over, check in with them periodically and see if there is a continued need. The families will forever be grateful for your continued care with their child and their family during a difficult time in their lives.

DAY 78

"My Father never stops working, and so I keep working, too."
JOHN 5:17 NCV

Lessons do not need to be over the top, but create experiences that help students understand the critical content. You do not have to recreate the wheel for every lesson throughout the school year. You are learning so much this year that it may not seem realistic to upgrade every single lesson in your units. Pick a content area or a unit that you could differentiate. Talk with others on your grade level, and maybe you could each update a lesson or two and share them with the other teachers. That way you can get multiple lessons for one unit that are engaging.

If you are able to pick one or two lessons this year, then the following year pick another two lessons. This way over time you have some great lessons that you have made more exciting or fun based on your students' needs. Make sure you know the critical standards for each unit because that is what your state test will cover in the spring. Find ways to make learning fun. Have the students act out or watch a video to gain some background knowledge. Turn dull review days into active games that get the students up and moving around. Eventually, you will have a bank of quality lessons that you can use year after year.

DAY 79

Thanks be to God for his inexpressible gift!

2 CORINTHIANS 9:15 ESV

Never pass on a class treat! My first teaching position was at a middle school, and I did not get a chance to enjoy a birthday treat unless I brought one into class. When I took a position at a third through fifth grade building, there were birthday treats and parties all of the time! I have noticed that many teachers throughout a year pass on the birthday treat. Many have great reasons including health restrictions, diet, and/or just full from lunch.

Students and their parents spend a lot of time and money to get treats for the class. It may not seem like a big deal, but take the gift anyway! This will make the student feel good that you enjoyed their snack. Take a few minutes to celebrate and maybe have a bin where students can pick out a small prize. If you definitely cannot and will not eat the treat, wait until the end of the day and give it to your spouse or significant other. No matter how full I am and how bad the food is for me, I take one anyway. It always makes the students feel great, and they taste good too!

DAY 80: REFLECTION AND PRAYER

DAY 81

"Trust yourself. You know more than you think you do."
—DR. SPOCK, *STAR TREK*

I like this Dr. Spock quote that is often used often used to encourage new parents but I think it applies to teachers as well. You now have just about a semester under your belt, and although you have much to learn about teaching, you have gleaned a lot of knowledge about your students, their families, and about yourself. You now have a pretty good idea about your strengths and your weaknesses as a teacher. Use this knowledge to help you and your students be successful during the second semester of the school year. If you are struggling with some of your classroom management, seek the support of a colleague who does it well, preferably someone that your student(s) have had in the past.

You are now sensing that "gut instinct" that teachers develop over time. You are beginning to see when students are struggling, and you can put interventions into place to help prevent them from falling between the cracks. Be observant because you are now able to tell how a student's days are going by their body language in the hallways. Make sure you talk to each student as they enter the classroom and let them know you care about them. You know more than you think you do. Play to your strengths and do not be afraid to ask for help when you need it.

DAY 82

Anxiety in a man's heart weighs him down,
but a good word makes him glad.

PROVERBS 12:25 ESV

Write a positive note to your students before they leave for Christmas break. For many, this is a time of anxiety and your words may help ease their stress. This is a great Christmas gift that you can give to your students no matter what age they are. This note should be personal and include a story or two about some great things they have done during the first semester, and where you have seen them grow so far this year. Many students dread going home for the holidays. Students in poverty are constantly reminded of their socio-economic status when they hear about all of the great gifts others have received over the break. For many, these students will be at home by themselves because their parents are working two jobs just to make ends meet.

This note will be a ray of God's light shining down on these students. You could mail it to them, so they actually have something to open from the mailbox. What kid does not like that! This note will give the students the strength to get through the holidays and know that when they return, they will come back to someone who cares deeply for them and wants them to be the best person they can be.

DAY 83

*"Six days you shall work, but on the seventh day you shall
rest. In plowing time and in harvest you shall rest."*

EXODUS 34:21 ESV

Try to avoid answering emails after 5:00 p.m. This can be hard for
some people. Whatever is in your inbox after 5:00 p.m. can wait
until 8:00 a.m. the next morning. Sure, there are certain times and
situations when it is essential to get back to a colleague. Try to avoid
sending emails to other staff members or responding to parents in the
evenings. The evening should be a time for your family and for your
colleagues to enjoy their families as well. This one was hard for me at
first because the app on my phone would send a notification when I
received a new email.

If other people know that you will be checking your email and
responding after 5:00 p.m., then they will continue to send emails and
expect responses through the evening. Draw a line for yourself for
when you will reply to others and stick to it. You have had a long day
working, and now it is time to take some time for yourself and your
family to recharge. The work will be there in the morning, and there
will always be work to be completed until June.

DAY 84

Therefore, since we are surrounded by such a great cloud of witnesses, let us throw off everything that hinders and the sin that so easily entangles. And let us run with perseverance the race marked out for us...

HEBREWS 12:1 NIV

Whether you are new to the teaching profession or have taught for several years, every school is different in how they operate. Talk with your coworkers, and do not be afraid to ask questions. Contact the previous year's teachers that have had your students and let them know how your students are progressing, and ask about strategies you could implement in your own classroom.

Visit other classrooms in the building and get some ideas on how master teachers have set up their rooms. Many have great organizational ideas and ways to make their room run more efficiently. Teachers Pay Teachers is also a great resource to look for ideas for your classroom. You will just need to set up an account. You will then pay for the PDF file, and then it is yours to use or edit how you wish. This will be worth checking out during various times throughout the year. If you have an interactive whiteboard, there are many websites as well such as SMART Exchange, which allows you to download lessons that work with SMART Notebook. Find out which teachers are using these programs and have them show you how it works.

DAY 85: REFLECTION AND PRAYER

DAY 86

"Seek first to understand, then to be understood."

—STEPHEN COVEY, AUTHOR,

SEVEN HABITS FOR HIGHLY EFFECTIVE PEOPLE

At some point, you will receive an email or a phone call from a parent or coworker that will make you upset. Your first instinct might be to email or call right back to defend yourself. One thing that I learned is to employ the twenty-four-hour rule regarding emails and phone calls. The twenty-four-hour rule is exactly that. When you get the urge to write back that nasty email, send a text message, or make that phone call, wait twenty-four hours to think about your response.

First, try to understand where they are coming from and what your response will be, then go ahead and email or call them back. Stay professional and try to listen to where your colleague is coming from. Sometimes, if you are working with a staff member, it is better to speak with them in person. Sarcasm and tone may be interpreted differently by the recipient through email or text. Go down the hallway and talk to them rather than email over a miscommunication. If you are having a hard time with a coworker or a parent, I guarantee there are other teachers in the building who have had similar struggles. Discuss the situation and ways to resolve the issue with your mentor. Their advice will help you with the staff or parents that you encounter.

DAY 87

Instruct the wise and they will be wiser still; teach the righteous and they will add to their learning.

PROVERBS 9:9 NIV

As an educator, you will need to be able to teach and model respect, responsibility, and accountability to your students. You also need to be there for them when they need you the most. The lack of classroom management or control causes loss of learning for all students in the classroom. Students will respect you more when you have a consistent structure in place for them. We all need boundaries and if they are not clear, then that will send mixed messages about what you will, and will not allow in your classroom.

With that being said, you will almost always have a student in your class that will push the limits, sometimes daily or hourly! If this is the case, you may need to work with this student on a behavior contract or plan that will help them be successful in your class. There are many ideas on the internet that come with templates, etc. Speak with your social worker as well, as there may already be a plan currently in place for this student. If you keep the bar high with your expectations, the students will hopefully reach it. Be consistent and do not give up.

DAY 88

Therefore, since we are surrounded by such a great cloud of witnesses, let us throw off everything that hinders and the sin that so easily entangles. And let us run with perseverance the race marked out for us…

Hebrews 12:1 NIV

There are going to be days when you wonder why you got into this profession. The pay is not great, you are going to be exhausted, and there will be days when you feel like you might not be making a difference. This is normal! You are not here for the money or fame, you are here to change the lives of the students you teach. If you are lacking in strength, patience, and energy, pray for these things each day. God knows your heart and wants to see you succeed in your calling. He will provide!

This "job" is a calling. Not many have the patience, endurance, or creativity in the spur of the moment to teach a classroom of students each day, month in and month out. Never underestimate or sell short the fact that you are in the profession for that reason—you have those skills. And if you do not, get out! You will know after the first couple of years if teaching is for you. The first year is the toughest, but the learning that takes place this year will shape the rest of your career. Soak it in!

DAY 89

"Work and get everything done during six days each week, but the seventh day is a day of rest to honor the LORD..."

EXODUS 20:9–10 NCV

S pend time with family and enjoy your weekends. This time of year gets really busy with events, report cards, grading, and somehow managing to fit teaching in as well! The semester can fill up quickly with other obligations, so enjoy the time you have with your family. Your family and friends are your support system, so it is important to spend some quality time with them. During this time together, make sure you tell them how much you appreciate them and their support during your first year(s) of teaching.

Over Christmas break, take some time to recharge and get back to the real meaning of Christmas. It is easy to get carried away with all of the "to-do" items before school gets out for the break. Now that it is almost here, carve out some time this break in quiet reflection on what this holiday season really means. He made the ultimate sacrifice out of love beginning on that Christmas Day. Remember His love and grace in your life. Pass it on to those you encounter each day!

DAY 90: REFLECTION AND PRAYER

Third Quarter

(January-March)

DAY 91

"Come to me, all you who are weary and burdened, and I will give you rest."

MATTHEW 11:28 NIV

Plan brain breaks. Take students on a walk or out to recess to get them up and moving. It is important to get some sunshine and fresh air rather than being indoors. Students can complete a journal entry about observations they are noticing from being outside. Have enough clipboards to go around or borrow some from another teacher, so papers do not blow away.

It is great to be outside, but some days are too busy, since Mother Nature does not always cooperate. Try to incorporate some brain breaks into your lessons. Find a spot in your day when you can break for thirty seconds to two minutes. There are many activities that you could try. One website that elementary students like is gonoodle.com. This website has many different songs that you can dance to. During a break, you can stretch, do jumping jacks, or get a quick drink. This is often enough to reset the students back into learning mode. Again, practicing the procedures and routines around brain breaks are vital as you want to get back to the content and back to learning. These breaks are great during testing sessions as well!

DAY 92

I will instruct you and teach you in the way you should go;
I will counsel you with my loving eye on you.

PSALM 32:8 NIV

Start your third quarter by going back over expectations, and continue to develop relationships with the students. Students are more interested and engaged with a teacher who they know cares about them. Just like the first few weeks of school, going over expectations is one of the best things you can do to have a productive and fun classroom in the coming weeks. Spend as much time as you need to going over your social contract, how to work respectfully in groups, and how to treat one another in the classroom. This can be done at any grade level, and this will set the tone for the rest of the quarter.

These activities are meant to be a refresher, so it should not take as long as it did at the beginning of the year. One possible way to incorporate writing is to have the students watch a video of students treating each other poorly, and another video of students working well in cooperative groups. Have students write down some of their observations, and at the end they can compare between the two. Students could produce some tangible examples on how they should work in collaborative groups. This activity could be referenced when you want to affirm and also remind students when they are not following the expectations.

DAY 93

But as for you, teach what accords with sound doctrine.

TITUS 2:1 ESV

You may be starting this semester with a whole new group of students. Reflect on what worked last semester, and what changes you can make for this semester to improve engagement and understanding. There is a big difference between the elementary and the secondary level. At the elementary level, you know the students and have built those relationships. Those relationships, so for these students, you can continue with relationship building.

At the secondary level, you will need to think back to that first week of school if you have a new group of students. Think about how you introduced students to your room, and start to establish routines, and build relationships. It is a good idea to remind students that no matter what happened last semester, they are starting off on a clean slate, and they are in charge of the rest of their school year. For some students, it might mean they will work on repairing broken relationships with students and staff. Be that support person for your students so they can be proud of their growth at the end of the year.

DAY 94

You will eat the fruit of your labor;
blessings and prosperity will be yours.

PSALM 128:2 NIV

Your lessons will not be perfect, but make sure your students are understanding the essential standards. Oftentimes in curriculum guides, there is way more content than you can pack into a fifty- to sixty-minute session with your students. There will be situations and events that will affect your instructional time at this point such as: student behaviors, emergency drills, class parties (if at the elementary level), and remediation of students who need extra support. You also do not want your high achieving students just sitting around waiting for you to finish, so you need to be prepared. All of this preparation takes time, so make every minute count.

Look to your colleagues for support. They may have the same time constraints as you. If they do, you could divide up the tasks for the unit. For example, one teacher who is excellent at extension activities could create something for the students who need an extra push in the content area. This could be a self-directed project, book study, etc. Another staff member who might specialize in remediation could come up with one to two remediation activities for struggling learners during the unit. The division of the workload will benefit everyone. A bonus is that you will already have the lessons ready to go for the following year!

DAY 95: REFLECTION AND PRAYER

DAY 96

Being strengthened with all power according to his glorious might so that you may have great endurance and patience...

COLOSSIANS 1:11 NIV

These months are tough! Keep persevering and moving forward, even when it feels like the end is so far away. The days are usually pretty short, and sometimes you will arrive to school in the dark, and leave in the dark! If you live in the northern states like Michigan, you will also be dealing with the elements of winter. One downside to winter is that you might not be able to have your students go outside due to low temperatures and wind chill. Then your worst fears come true...INDOOR RECESS! This time of year can be pretty chaotic, but try to hang out with your students every once in a while during this time. They will like spending time with you outside of your role as the teacher.

This time of year is critical for student learning. The state testing window for most districts is after spring break, so you will want to get as much in as possible. There will be some roadblocks to this, so you need to be flexible. One barrier will be snow days if you have them. They are great; however, they do take away a day from new learning. Enjoy those days and use them to recharge for the next day. Another roadblock will be illness. During the winter, many students will be sick, so be understanding, and try to work with students to help them get caught up. Remember to try to keep the lessons engaging and students moving around with plenty of breaks during class.

DAY 97

This is the day that the LORD has made;
let us rejoice and be glad in it.

PSALM 118:24 ESV

E mbrace and celebrate snow days (if you live in the North). What great days these are if you are lucky enough to get them! Snow days are fantastic because your lesson plans are already set up, and it is a free day to enjoy with your family (minus shoveling snow of course). Checking your email is a good idea because you may have to reschedule a meeting or other event you had planned that was foiled by Mother Nature.

Most students really love snow days, almost as much as we do! For some parents and students, this can be a stressful day. Often parents still have to go to work, or they might be forced to take a day off. Students also might not like being at home, and the change of routine can really affect them. Typically, snow days are only one or two days in a row and then students can get back to learning. Try to check in with your students and give some extra attention to those you feel might need it. Spend some time with your class when you return just to see how they spent their time. Students will be eager to share, and it will allow your students to bond together more as a group.

DAY 98

In everything set them an example by doing what is good.
In your teaching show integrity, seriousness.

TITUS 2:7 NIV

Continue building positive relationships with your students. This is the time of year when you want to keep instilling respect, integrity, and honesty with your students. As with many of us, when the days are cloudy, and there may be snow everywhere, we could get a little down. In the winter, people are more susceptible to depression, anxiety, and loneliness. This can happen with your students too. Make sure that during these months you continue to help build up students who might need extra encouragement.

Schools often embrace a character trait to focus on for an entire month. Recently, our school looked at integrity. Each class had some activities for that month related to integrity. This could easily be tied into the regular curriculum and does not have to be something extra to design. We showed videos and read stories about inspiring about students who showed great integrity through some challenging times. We often have students write about these stories afterward to see how they could apply this to their own lives. Make it fun, but make sure students continue to respect themselves and each other to ensure you have a safe classroom to learn and grow.

DAY 99

"When I stand before God at the end of my life, I would hope that I would not have a single bit of talent left, and could say, I used everything you gave me."

—ERMA BOMBECK

Work at differentiating a few more of your lessons. You now have a good idea what subject or unit you enjoy teaching to your students. Try adapting some of those lessons for your struggling and high achieving learners. For example, if you know your next math unit will be around twelve to fifteen lessons in length, shoot for one to two towards the end of the unit that you can focus on differentiating well. Why not try to differentiate every single lesson? As some of my colleagues would say, "Treat it like you are eating an elephant." You have a lot going on, and you are relatively new at differentiating lessons. Adapting a few lessons will give you a sense of what works for your students and what needs to be changed.

This does not have to be an entirely new lesson for your learners. You will have groups of students who are in very different places. In general, minor tweaks to the curriculum and adjustments will help most struggling learners. Your high achieving students can work on applying this new skill in more real-world situations. If you take a little at a time, over the next few years, you will have more of these lessons in your toolbox. And even more, if you are able to collaborate with a teammate!

DAY 100: REFLECTION AND PRAYER

DAY 101

Let no one despise you for your youth, but set the believers an example in speech, in conduct, in love, in faith, in purity.

1 TIMOTHY 4:12 ESV

Make sure that students are doing more of the thinking, talking, and working than you are. Part of a student-centered classroom is turning over some to most of the responsibility to the students. This can be hard for some teachers because they have always known complete autonomy over how the lessons were going to be delivered. The students have a worksheet, and the teacher or expert provided the information expecting that the students retain it. This type of content delivery is necessary for some lessons, but it does not have to be the norm.

Try to build ways in which your students can interact with the experiences, and give them some choices. Start with only two to three options, all of which are standards that they must cover by the end of the unit. This flexibility helps to ensure that all of the content will be included. The students are usually more willing to complete the work when they have chosen the assignment. In one of these assignments, try to be a facilitator of information. Challenge students by asking questions to their group and encourage discourse to solve the problem. Give the students resources to use, but do not give too much information. The students will walk away from these lessons with a more profound knowledge of the content.

DAY 102

*But those who hope in the Lord will renew their strength.
They will soar on wings like eagles; they will run and not
grow weary, they will walk and not be faint.*

ISAIAH 40:31 NIV

These are the slow months. Less daylight, colder temperatures, flu season, and state assessment prep could make for a grumpy classroom. Try to find ways to lighten up the mood in the classroom. Brain breaks, academic scavenger hunts, a ten-minute yoga routine in the morning—ANYTHING to switch things up and get the students moving. This will help you and your students look forward to coming to school each day. I try to share a joke of the day with the students to lighten the mood on these darker days. It is necessary to take care of our minds and bodies during this time of year because we are all a little more susceptible to getting sick, and we can become irritable with one another.

This can be a tough time for teachers as well. It is just as vital for you to take care of yourself as much as taking care of your students. Make sure you are getting plenty of rest during this time, so you are not running out of patience with some of your more trying students. Try a new brain break each day with your students, and get up and participate with them. This will help you refresh even if it is only for a minute. Have fun with your students during this busy assessment season.

DAY 103

"Ask, and it will be given to you; seek, and you will find; knock, and it will be opened to you."

MATTHEW 7:7 ESV

Ask for volunteers to help in your classroom. These adults do not have to be parents of students in your class. Adults are great to have in your classroom because they might be able to make a connection with a student who might need a positive influence in their life. Sometimes, students just need to hear information from other adults than their teacher. Invite them to read to your students. Parents or other community members could help tutor students a couple of days a week. There are many church members and former teachers who would love to go into the school and help out. These folks just need to be asked!

When you have other adults in the classroom, think about the time you will have them, and how they can be a productive part of your class. It is not enjoyable for them or productive if they are just standing around while you lecture. Work out a schedule, so that when the adult comes into the classroom, they can jump right in with helping students. Volunteers are able to work with students who might need extra help during your instructional time. This will allow you to focus on enriching and differentiating your lessons for other groups in your classroom.

DAY 104

"By failing to prepare, you are preparing to fail."

—BENJAMIN FRANKLIN

C ontinue to work on being organized and prepared. This daily discipline will help you to stay on top of your grading and curriculum work. One way to stay prepared and organized is to grade assignments that need to be recorded, and then return them to the students. Students need feedback on their work, and a score does not tell them a whole lot. Take some time if you can, to write a comment or two about what they have done well and where to improve. Grading assignments as they come in will help prevent the accumulation of large stacks at the end of the week for you to complete over the weekend.

Start to develop, if you have not already, either an online or a hard copy of your lessons by the unit. I have them stored on the computer listed by lesson number no matter what content area. This way when I look at the lesson the following year, I can tweak the assignment as necessary, but not have to redo the whole thing. The benefit of having it online is that you can send it immediately through your learning management system (LMS) via Google Classroom, Moodle, Schoology, etc. Most lessons can be done this way without having to stand by a copy machine. If you have the resources, take advantage of them.

DAY 105: REFLECTION AND PRAYER

DAY 106

This is the day that the LORD has made;
let us rejoice and be glad in it.

PSALM 118:24 ESV

Celebrate growth daily. There are many ways to celebrate growth on student goals in your classroom. One way is to have the students set personal goals for the week, month, or grading period in your class. The students can then graph the results based on the goals they have set for themselves. For example, if students set a goal for themselves to read 100 minutes in a week, they could graph how many minutes they read each day, and add it up at the end of the week. Make sure that you make it a point to acknowledge the student for making progress towards their goals! Other students may need a tangible reward for when they reach their goal.

When working with your students to set goals, try the SMART goals method. Goals need to be specific measurable, achievable in the amount of time specified, realistic, and timely. There are a lot of useful resources out there on the web for setting and tracking SMART goals. I would suggest giving students a data tracking sheet where they can visually see their goal progress. This will help provide them with a target to meet their goal. Later on, they can look back on their previous goal as an example. Walk through the first one with your students, so they know your expectations. After doing a few of these, students will be able to set goals and track the progress on their own.

DAY 107

May our Lord Jesus Christ himself and God our Father encourage you and strengthen you in every good thing you do and say.

2 THESSALONIANS 2:17 NCV

A significant part of teaching is helping to develop children into the amazing people that God intended them to be. Think about how you can incorporate some real-world conversations with your students to help them not only to be critical thinkers, but to become citizens of a bigger world than just themselves.

One person that I absolutely admire is one of our fourth grade teachers. He is a man after God's own heart, and daily he shares experiences and lessons with his students who will carry on with them long after fourth grade. He teaches in a public school, but his teachings could be applied in any setting. At the end of every school day, they have a time when they discuss big issues; talk about what it means to be honest; to have integrity; to be humble; and showing grace to others. These students live out these principles by visiting residents in a local nursing home once a month to play games, listen to music, and just have conversations with them. It brightens the residents' day and gives the students a whole new perspective on life through a service learning experience. These experiences help to make long-lasting, positive impressions on these students.

DAY 108

*For lack of guidance a nation falls,
but victory is won through many advisers.*

PROVERBS 11:14 NIV

B y this time, you have identified your students strengths and weaknesses. Play to the strengths (enrichment) and work at the weaknesses (remediation). This is an excellent opportunity for you to be able to work in small groups with students who need an extra push, or with students who did not understand today's lesson. If this sort of time is not built into your daily schedule, try to be flexible to create some time, forty to forty-five minutes, or so dedicated for this purpose. At the secondary level, this is typically a study hall or supports class. If you are able to build in this precious time, use it wisely with researched-based interventions.

Talk to your school psychologist, special education team, and your mentor about research-based interventions that would work well for your students. There are many out there, but you want to use the ones that will give you more return for your time that you have them. Some of your students might be out of the classroom to receive other services, such as reading or math support. This is an excellent time to start documenting what you are doing to see what is working and what is not. Collect data and take it to your special education team if you are thinking that a student might need more intensive interventions.

DAY 109

Let the wise listen and add to their learning,
and let the discerning get guidance...

Proverbs 1:5 NIV

It is okay that things have come up this year that your education courses did not prepare you for. That is why this book has been designed for you, the new teacher. The theory, lectures, and pedagogy classes are great at building a foundation, but the theory becomes reality when the rubber hits the road during that first year of teaching. Hopefully, your student teaching experience was excellent, and you were able to glean knowledge from your supervising teacher, professors, and administrators. Rest assured knowing that all teachers have gone through this and survived!

The best way to be proactive about any future situations that might arise is through conversations with your mentor or other colleagues. Buy them a coffee one morning before school, and ask to pick their brain for a few minutes about the challenges of a first-year teacher. Ask them about how they handle second semester situations, and how evaluations are typically handled at the end of the year. It is nice to have some time to think about these situations and be ready for them when they come. Do not forget that coffee!

DAY 110: REFLECTION AND PRAYER

DAY 111

She dresses herself with strength and makes her arms strong.

PROVERBS 31:17 ESV

This is a great time of year to get into the gym or start going for walks. Exercise is one activity that you might find to be a good stress reliever, especially after a long day at school. Many view the new year as a good time to begin an exercise routine. This is not a bad idea after eating all of that delicious food over Christmas break! Taking care of your body is essential. When you get enough sleep, and sufficient exercise, you will be able to handle your job easier on tough days with students as well as the everyday demands of teaching.

A great free way to get some exercise is to go for a walk. It is a little harder in the winter, but no matter what you decide to do for some exercise, pick a time that works the best for you. I have three young children, and our after-school time is hectic, to say the least! We play for a little while, make dinner, clean up, and then start the going to bed routine. There is not a lot of time or energy for a workout after all of that! The best time for me is in the morning before school. It is harder in the winter because it is so warm under those blankets, but I felt renewed when I went to the gym or for a walk before school started. I just seemed more relaxed and ready for the day. Whatever you decide, keep it consistent and have fun!

DAY 112

For this is the message that you have heard from the beginning, that we should love one another.

1 JOHN 3:11 ESV

Do something with your coworkers that is not work related. This is a great way to connect with your colleagues and get to know them on a personal level too. It is important to build relationships with those around you. You never know when you might be able to be a blessing to them.

In order to get to know each other better, once a month, there was an open invitation to anyone who wanted to go to hang out after work at a local restaurant to enjoy some good food and company. We called it our Friday Afternoon Club (FAC). I really appreciated and looked forward to the FAC time we spent together because did not talk about school. Even though that was the connection among all of us, we took the time to listen and get to know each other each week. I learned so much about my colleagues that I would not have otherwise known. Carve out some time to spend with your colleagues, and continue to cultivate the relationships with these special people throughout the year.

DAY 113

"By this all people will know that you are my disciples, if you have love for one another."

JOHN 13:35 ESV

Try to get to know your administration better. Their lives matter too. They have a very tough job, and they have lives also outside of school. Take a minute to get to know them. Follow up in a few weeks to see how everything is going. This may not seem like a big thing to do, but stopping in for a couple of minutes and asking how things are going will help to build a positive rapport. This could be as simple as asking if they had a good weekend or asking how their kids are doing.

Our administrators have many important decisions they make behind the scenes that we do not even know about, and without this work, our schools would not run as smoothly as they do. Take some time to pray for their leadership and their families, as they too are working through busy seasons in their lives.

DAY 114

*The LORD replied, "My Presence will go
with you, and I will give you rest."*

EXODUS 33:14 NIV

These are some long months and a mental health day may be needed to help you recharge. This is not a day because you are sick, but a just-for-you relaxing kind of day. Find something that you want to do and go out and do it! Enjoy having longer than twenty minutes to eat lunch and not checking emails. Catch up on some housework or do nothing at all! Hopefully, this day will allow you to be rejuvenated and ready to help your students.

Most school districts have a policy on how many days you can take off, so make sure you read over your contract. There might be stipulations regarding taking off the Friday before a break, such as spring break or Christmas. Also, make sure you have a reliable substitute to take your class for the day. Try and meet this person beforehand to go over the day if possible. This will help alleviate any stress knowing your class is in good hands so you can relax or go on an adventure. These days are revitalizing because it is another mini break to look forward to during these long months.

DAY 115: REFLECTION AND PRAYER

DAY 116

When you have many kinds of troubles, you should be full of joy, because you know that these troubles test your faith, and this will give you patience.

JAMES 1:2–3 NIV

S ometimes, a student needs a break from your class to reset or to chill out for a moment. I have had many times when a student was struggling to stay focused, or were starting to distract others for various reasons. I would send them on an errand. There have been years when I really could not leave the room even to make a copy, so having a student run to the office for a minute to help make some copies was a big help. We had an understanding that when they took at chill out, the student just needed a minute to refocus. This may become a regular necessity for some students to get a break from the classroom.

If you do need to incorporate this routine for a student, make sure you talk to some of the other teachers to make sure it is ok with them and that they know the plan for the student. It is important that the student know that there are parameters around this "chill out" time or errand that they are sent to run for you. Task and return to the classroom immediately. Students may often get "lost" wandering the hallways, which will take away from their learning and your instruction with other students. Once those expectations are in place, they will get a much-needed break, and you will have a helper too.

DAY 117

I can do all things through him who strengthens me.

PHILIPPIANS 4:13 ESV

Now that you have a semester under your belt, try to improve on how you can be more efficient for next year. Next year's planning will be much easier when you make some quick notes about what has gone well, and ways that you can tweak your current lessons. There are some great programs out there that can help you with data collection and grading.

One way to help yourself in the immediate future is to have students grade their own papers and make corrections when appropriate. This is a way that students can have immediate feedback on whether they understand the material. If students know they are able to make corrections on their work, then they can focus more on learning the concepts and problem solving with peers. Many assignments such as tests and quizzes should be done by the teacher, but daily tasks should be partly on the student as a way to take ownership of their learning. You will know soon if you have to adjust this, if students are acing their homework but showing poor scores on their assessments.

DAY 118

I was given mercy so that in me, the worst of all sinners,
Christ Jesus could show that he has patience without limit.

1 TIMOTHY 1:16 NCV

K now that at times things will be difficult, but all of the difficult times are worth the impact you are making on so many lives. As a role model, you have the chance to encourage and uplift your students as soon as school starts! Throughout the day, you also have opportunities to be a shining light to students in need. There will be tough days, but your students will have rough days too and will be looking for your guidance.

It is so important to build relationships with your students and maintain them all year. Your students will be looking for support from you (even if they do not show it) because they may not have a support system at home. One student, in particular, comes to mind. This student's family was homeless, and they lived somewhere new each week. This put a significant strain on my student because she did not know where they were going to spend the night when they left school that day. These problems make me so humble when I think about having a warm home and a loving, supportive family to return to each day after school. Be a positive role model for these students and give them encouraging words daily.

DAY 119

Return to your rest, my soul,
for the Lord has been good to you.

PSALM 116:7 NIV

Sometimes, you have to leave school at school. It is easy to get wrapped up in lesson planning and grading, but keep a social life! It is especially important to keep in contact with your friends and family. Try and reconnect with some friends you have not heard from in a while. I received a book from one of my students called *3 Day Getaways-Michigan Back Roads*. This was the perfect gift at the perfect time when I needed a break from the demands of the school year. Sometimes, you need to get out of town and go for a drive!

Set a goal for yourself this week to do something fun that is *not* school related. You have been putting in a lot of time and energy at school, and it is time to recharge a little bit. Call up a few friends and try a new restaurant, go for a hike, see a movie, whatever can get you out of your house and classroom for a little while. It is important to nurture these relationships with your friends and family because they are your support system. You will need to lean on them for advice as well as be a kind listening ear during your first years of teaching.

DAY 120: REFLECTION AND PRAYER

DAY 121

The soul of the sluggard craves and gets nothing,
while the soul of the diligent is richly supplied.

PROVERBS 13:4 ESV

S tay organized. If you are lucky, you will teach this subject or grade level again, and it will make the next year go smoother if you can easily locate all of your lessons. Teachers have many different systems that they like to use to organize their curriculum. Some teachers like binders with each subject area that they teach, and then divide this up into units of study. In these units, they have a master copy of any homework assignments as well as formative and summative assessments. I have found that keeping a copy of as many assignments as I can in a digital file can be more convenient to use over time.

Putting files in a cloud-based system allows you to work on these documents wherever you are, and you do not have to carry a heavy binder with you. These digital copies will enable you to quickly make changes to your lessons and share them with students. When I have students who miss a day or two of class, I can email the assignments to the parents or students, so they can work on them. This type of organizational system has been beneficial for me. This filing system helps to create a more organized and convenient way to see all of the classes that I am teaching in one location.

DAY 122

For we are His workmanship, created in Christ Jesus for good works, which God prepared beforehand that we should walk in them.

EPHESIANS 2:10 NKJV

Find ways to get the parents into the classroom. These volunteers can observe presentations, help with experiments, or assist students as they edit their writing. The parents do not need any formal training to help out in the classroom. All volunteers are required to complete a volunteer form, and background check, etc., to ensure the safety of the students. When volunteers arrive, introduce them to the students and orient them with the classroom. Thank the volunteers and let them know how much you appreciate their willingness to help.

I have had parents in our classes, and they have walked away not only with a better understanding of the curriculum, but also an appreciation for what we do on a daily basis. We are living out our faith each day by being counselors, nurses, teachers, motivators, and friends to our students. There are not too many careers that give you the opportunity to impact lives on a daily basis. Reaching out to parents and community members will allow others to see how your classroom and building are making a positive impact for children in the community.

DAY 123

Our faces, then, are not covered. We all show the Lord's glory, and we are being changed to be like him.

2 CORINTHIANS 3:18 NIV

Teaching is, in my mind, the noblest of professions. So much goes into preparation for it, and it never stops. Training young minds to be the citizens of tomorrow is giving society a gift that not many can provide. There are many surveys out there regarding job satisfaction, and time again teaching others is shown as one of the most rewarding professions out there. Seeing that "Aha!" moment for a student and giving them the tools to be critical thinkers makes me want to come back day after day to serve my of students.

It is important to remember that you are doing meaningful work for your community. You are building up leaders for tomorrow, and this does not always come with excellent compensation. One day, I actually sat down and calculated how much I made per hour that I worked. I took into account grading on weeknights, and all of the other obligations that a teacher has when the students are not in the classroom. I cannot remember the number exactly, but it was definitely under minimum wage! Of course, there are other perks to teaching such as great time off, etc. But we did not go into teaching for money or time off, you are here to impact the lives of students each day.

DAY 124

*For everything there is a season, and a time
for every matter under heaven...*

ECCLESIASTES 3:1 ESV

Change the schedule a little to make lessons new and engaging. If you are at the elementary level, this is a little easier for you to do because you might have larger blocks of instructional time throughout the day. At the secondary level, you may want to consider changing how you introduce or close the lesson to get the students engaged in the topic, or to have an exit ticket as an informal assessment for the students on their way out of the door. Mixing up the order of the day might be a good way to help students in particular content areas. You also have to think about some of your students who might have a hard time with any changes. If you do make changes, make sure these students know ahead of time so they can prepare for it.

As you look at your achievement data and behavior management plan, moving certain subjects to different times of the day might be helpful. We often saw behaviors at the end of the day. After some discussion and looking at the students grades, we decided to move math to the beginning of the day and reading to the end of the day. The students responded well to this change and were ready to learn at the beginning of the day. We started seeing grades improve, behaviors decrease, and students appreciated having some time to relax and read their library books for a few minutes at the end of the day. Take a look at your schedule and see where you might be able to make some positive changes for you and your students.

DAY 125: REFLECTION AND PRAYER

DAY 126

Jesus often withdrew to lonely places and prayed.

LUKE 5:16 NIV

There is a lot that goes into the first year of teaching. Sometimes there are long hours, tough students, learning new curriculum, and trying to balance your life at home. Spend time in prayer each day, not only for your students and their families, but also your own family. Ask for energy and strength to be a good spouse and friend to those around you. Using up your tank of patience at school is easy. There are many times that you cannot fill it back up on your own. Ask for help!

I do not typically like to talk about school when I get home because I want to focus on my family, but there are indeed instances when a listening ear and objective opinion can make all the difference in the world. Your spouse/significant other can listen while you vent about a stressful day that you have had. It is normal to have bad days, but do not be the only one venting and try not to do it every day. Be an active listener to your spouse/significant other because they also need to be able to come to you for support as well.

DAY 127

*And this I pray, that your love may abound still
more and more in real knowledge and all discernment.*

PHILIPPIANS 1:9 NASB

E njoy your students. They now know what you expect of them, so take time to really enjoy being with your students. You have stayed consistent with your expectations since the beginning of the year, and hopefully, that consistency and routine is starting to pay off in your classroom. This is the best time of year because it can be very productive and fun for you and your students. Raise the bar for your students during this time. You know what they are able to achieve, so challenge them. You will be surprised at the results! Have fun incentives for the students when they meet the class goals. Typically, there is a lot of growth during this quarter because students are used to the routines and there are less breaks this time of year.

Remember to continue to have individual conversations with your students about how they are doing outside of school. Get to know your students on a deeper level, especially the ones who are still having a hard time. You might need to change or update the behavior or work completion contract with them to get some buy-in. Compromise is a healthy part of a relationship. Be flexible when you can with your students. When you give them some choice on assignments, you will get quality results, and they will have more flexibility in completing their work.

DAY 128

Blessed is the one who perseveres under trial because, having stood the test, that person will receive the crown of life that the Lord has promised to those who love him.

JAMES 1:12 NIV

Some days you may feel like a failure, or you may feel like you are not getting things across to your students: This is perfectly normal! Perseverance certainly pays off with students throughout the school year. I have worked with many students that show significant behaviors at school as well as at home. Showing students that you care for them means holding them accountable for their actions at school. Hopefully, over the course of the year, you will see many gains academically and socially for your students. There might be years that you do not see the fruit of your labor during the school year, but down the road, it will make a difference.

You never know when a student will come up to you and thank you for taking the time to help them. I recently had a student come up to me who was my student a few years ago. They said that because of the time I spent with him and helped with his school work, he was now on the honor roll and doing great. He now has a goal to attend college and be the first person in his home to graduate!

DAY 129

*All things work together for good, for those
who are called according to his purpose.*

ROMANS 8:28 ESV

S tudents need someone who will encourage and believe in them. Many years ago, I taught a career unit where students were able to pick a dream job, research it, and then present to the class. During one of the beginning sessions of the project, I met with each student about their career choice. One student confided in me and said, "I want to be a fireman, but no one in my house has ever graduated from high school. I don't know if I can do it." I simply told him, "I believe in you. If you want it bad enough, you can do it."

Recently, that same student sent me a photograph of himself. I was amazed at how he had grown, but that was overshadowed by the pride I felt by seeing him in his graduation gown. Underneath the picture was what I told him a few years prior: "I believe in you. If you want it bad enough, you can do it." You never know what impact you might have on your students. You might not see it this year, but down the road, the seeds you sow will hopefully come to fruition for your students.

DAY 130: REFLECTION AND PRAYER

DAY 131

Through him all things were made; without him nothing was made that has been made.

JOHN 1:3 NIV

Brainstorm experiential field trips. Elementary and secondary students alike will remember these experiences you gave them. Each year, the elementary school in which I teach takes the fifth grade class to a nearby university. Many of these students have never been talked to about college before, let alone step foot on a college campus; so this was a big deal for our students. We had a blast at the university! We rented the fieldhouse so students could enjoy the pool, basketball and racquetball courts, and other activities. We ate lunch on the lawn and took a walk around campus to see the different classrooms.

The conversations that came up during this visit with my small group of students was much more than I would ever get out of them in the classroom. Many left saying, "I want to go to college now. I'm not sure what I want to be yet when I grow up, but I know where I want to go!" That is pretty powerful coming from a fifth grade student. Give your students opportunities to learn from community members and exploring nature. You certainly do not have to rent a fieldhouse, but come up with something for students to remember and think about for years to come.

DAY 132

Open your mouth for the mute, for the rights of all who are destitute. Open your mouth, judge righteously, defend the rights of the poor and needy.

Proverbs 31:8–9 ESV

B e an advocate for your students. Many of you may see the same students for six hours a day. In a week, that is around thirty hours that you are with someone's child. Often teachers see students more than the parents interact with their children during a day. You, as a teacher, must do what is right for each student. There might be students with special needs in your classroom that need accommodations across various settings. As a teacher, it is your job and their right to have their needs met. Students and their families may need extra support outside of school because they are homeless, struggling with bills, appointments, etc. Talk to your colleagues about how you can refer these families to agencies within the community.

This could also mean standing up for a student whom you suspect might be neglected or abused. If you suspect anything is going on with students or if they tell you things that are suspicious, you are a mandated reporter of that information. Talk to your administrator and counselor/social worker to let them know what you have overheard or observed. They will help guide you when you need to file a report. Always report any incidence to your administrators.

DAY 133

We are hard pressed on every side, but not crushed; perplexed, but not in despair; persecuted, but not abandoned; struck down, but not destroyed.

2 CORINTHIANS 4:8–9 NIV

As you teach, you learn what works and what does not work in your classroom. Sometimes it may just take trial and error. Keep pushing through, and know that you are making an incredible difference in the lives of so many! Write in the margins of your lesson plans, or take some notes on what is working and what is not. This will be valuable information for the next year.

On the days where you feel like nothing is going right, make sure you take some extra time for yourself to recharge. Remember that tomorrow is another day and that your family and friends are there for you. On your ride home, or the next day on the way to school, think about how the day could turn around for you and your students. Think of reasons why the students may be acting the way they are since there is usually an underlying reason. Make sure you reconnect and follow up with students that had a hard day today or yesterday. Let them know you still care about them, and you want them to be successful.

DAY 134

Repent, then, and turn to God, so that your sins may be wiped out, that times of refreshing may come from the Lord...

ACTS 3:19 NIV

Every day, hundreds of thousands of new parents bring home babies that they have no idea how to care for, and despite that, mankind has persisted for thousands of years. This is the same for teaching. You are going to do fine, and when you make the guaranteed goofs, it is not the end of the world. Embrace the mistakes you make and will make in your career. If you are not making mistakes, then you and your students will not be learning and pushed to think deeper. Let them know when you made a mistake and students will respect you for telling them when you made a mistake; and realize that you are human too.

Students are very resilient and will forgive you for your mistakes. This is an excellent opportunity to talk about forgiveness and grace. Think of our Heavenly Father and His mercy towards us. No matter what we have done, if we come to Him and tell of our mistakes, He will shape us to learn from them. The same is true for teaching. Take each mistake, no matter how painful, as a way to improve your craft. The key is to take notes and learn from others mistakes as well. Learn and grow as a community in your school, and your students will follow in your footsteps.

DAY 135: REFLECTION AND PRAYER

Fourth Quarter

(MARCH-JUNE)

DAY 136

He will yet fill your mouth with laughter
and your lips with shouts of joy.

Job 8:21 NIV

Maintain your sense of humor. Laughing helps to relieve stress, and laughing with your students them know that you have a fun side as well. I recently attended a conference presentation by Marcia Tate, who is a leader in educational development for children. As she talked throughout her keynote, she described how children learned and that worksheets do not build dendrites. Another tip that she gave us was to laugh. She said that we should tell jokes in class and keep things light. When students are relaxed and smiling, they are more able to learn. After I went to this conference, I began to use a joke of the day in my classroom. The kids really look forward to this every day no matter what age level I am working with. It is just a great way to start a class!

It's also important to laugh with your coworkers. Telling a funny story of what your student did in class is great because you can all relate. You may even want to start a running notebook of funny things that have happened throughout your year! During some of the harder days, you can look back and laugh at some of the funny moments throughout the school year.

DAY 137

We give thanks to God always for all of you,
constantly mentioning you in our prayers...

THESSALONIANS 1:2 ESV

This is a busy time of year and it moves fast! Make sure to make time for yourself and your family. During the school year, my wife and family have been incredibly supportive through all of the meetings, conferences, and other duties that I have outside of school hours. Teachers often coach or help with other after-school activities, and this takes time away from your friends and family. Make sure that your support system how much you have appreciated their support and encouragement throughout this year.

Try and plan some time during the school week when you and your spouse/significant other can get away for a few hours and not think about work or other stressors in your life. This may mean you will have to get a babysitter. You may be exhausted when you go out that night because you have had a long day, but it is time well spent. It is worth it to treat your partner to a special night to thank them for all they have done to continually love and support you. Next year, try and make time each month to spend with friends and family who have supported you over the year. I promise the work will not go anywhere, and it will get done...just not tonight!

DAY 138

Let your eyes look directly forward,
and your gaze be straight before you.

Proverbs 4:25 ESV

Continue to model what is appropriate and be very intentional in reteaching correct behaviors throughout the building. Go back to that social contract that you introduced during the first few weeks of school. Just like you reminded your students of routines and expectations, have this conversation again with them to keep everyone on the same page. Students at this point in the year might start to make some poor choices. I had one student who would always self-sabotage his work at the end of the year. I talked to his previous teachers, and they said he did the same thing in their class. He performed well all year, but at the end of the year, he ended up struggling in all of his classes.

In your discussion with the students regarding expectations, you might compare the year to running a race. Perseverance and growth over the year are what matters, and over time people will not remember a students by what grades they received in math class or biology. We will remember how the students persevered against adversity when things seemed hard. Discuss with students that running this race is like a marathon, and finishing strong will give them hope and strength knowing that they are ready to face challenges in the future.

DAY 139

Finally, brothers, whatever is true, whatever is honorable,
whatever is just, whatever is pure, whatever is lovely,
whatever is commendable, if there is any excellence, if there is
anything worthy of praise, think about these things.

PHILIPPIANS 4:8 ESV

Stay positive. You are making a difference! At this point in the school year, the weather is starting to turn around, and you can see the light at the end of the tunnel. The spring rains and flowers remind us that we begin new and have a fresh start. Keep this outlook with your students throughout the end of the school year. Help them to remember that they can make it a great day or not. The choice is theirs to make.

As for you and your teaching, stay positive about yourself, and think about all of the growth you have made this school year. There have definitely been some blown lesson plans and days where nothing seems to have gone right. That does not stop after the first year of teaching! Remember to laugh, help one another, and lift each other up when your colleagues need it. Do not give up on your students. They need everything you have until that last day of school. It always helps me to get outside during my lunch period to get some fresh air and get a little sunshine. This helps brighten my day, and it is a much-needed distraction that allow me to reset in order to be ready for the afternoon. The end of the year is near, and you can do it!

DAY 140: REFLECTION AND PRAYER

DAY 141

*The heart of man plans his way, but
the LORD establishes his steps.*

PROVERBS 16:9 ESV

Give yourself a little more leeway in the fourth quarter. School is finishing up, and students are getting excited about summer. Keep those routines going, and establish some normalcy towards the end of the school year. Also, give yourself some room to try out some new activities that will get your students up and moving around. Look at your upcoming lessons for the last few weeks, and see where you could incorporate some movement into your lessons. Your students are almost as stir crazy for summer as you are!

There are many great resources available to you for hands-on activities. Some of the best resources are your colleagues. Try and team up with one or two other teachers to have a combined lesson where students might be able to mix in with other students, and work together from another classroom. We once had a mobile farm lab come to our school, and each class was able to go out to the lab and work with the scientist on extracting wheat germ from seeds. It was a pretty awesome way to tie in the science lesson from class! This does take some planning, especially if you are having guests come in. Plan well, and this could be something you could incorporate for years to come to enrich your curriculum while getting those students up and moving.

DAY 142

Watch yourselves, so that you may not lose what we have worked for, but may win a full reward.

2 JOHN 1:8 ESV

B e prepared for behaviors to spike during this time of year. Give the students your best everyday, and the students will know that you care. Talk to these students previous teachers as you have done throughout the year and see how these students finished out the year. They might have some insight into ways to keep them engaged and finish the year strong. If you are proactive about this, then you might be able to prevent or minimize the behaviors before they arise.

Incentives may be a good way to keep your "frequent fliers" out of the office toward the end of the year. Talk to these students and come up with a game plan for how both of you would like the end of the year to go. You could plan a pizza party with them and a few of their friends, take the student out to lunch, extra recess, etc. Reach out to these students in a positive way so they know that you are trying to help, and will do whatever you can to help them succeed. We all want the students to finish the year on a high note and be proud of themselves when looking back on the school year.

DAY 143

A disciple is not above his teacher, but everyone when he is fully trained will be like his teacher.

LUKE 6:40 ESV

K now that as hard as you try, you might not reach every student. That is why they leave your classroom and get the opportunity to learn from others. It takes a village to raise a child. This was probably the hardest part of becoming a new teacher for me. You work so hard all year long pouring everything you have into these students, and yet many still struggle. Or, perhaps you did not make that connection that would make a positive lasting impression on that student. Remember that you are a piece of their puzzle, and a stop in their journey to adulthood.

While you may think you have not made a difference this year with one or two of your students, you have instilled in them (whether they liked it or not) a sense of accountability, and integrity through your words and actions. Hopefully, down the road they will look back and begin to reap the reward of the seeds you planted throughout this school year. Many of them may come back to share with you their success stories, but others will not, and you will be left wondering. Do not worry, you have made a difference!

DAY 144

*Commit your work to the LORD,
and your plans will be established.*

PROVERBS 16:3 ESV

This might seem harsh, but do not waste time. The parents are trusting you, and sometimes paying a lot of money for you to educate their children. Toward the end of the semester, it can be hard to keep yourself and your students motivated. Look for creative ways to cover the necessary standards to keep pace with your curriculum with your department or grade level.

One way to make your lessons more interactive is through project-based learning. You could have experts from the community and guest speakers come in to your class after a culminating project. One example of project-based learning is building catapults. This is an exciting way for students to work on their building, collaborating, and problem-solving skills. Students get only twelve popsicle sticks and sixteen rubber bands, and they have to watch a video on how to make the catapult. A way to extend the project at the end is to have an engineer come to the class to get the students interested in STEM careers. These projects help build excitement, and keep lessons fun for you and your students.

DAY 145: REFLECTION AND PRAYER

DAY 146

I am the good shepherd; I know my sheep, and my sheep know me—just as the Father knows me and I know the Father— and I lay down my life for the sheep.

JOHN 10:14–15 NIV

Stay grounded. Schools love to cram every possible event into the last quarter of the school year: field day, assessments, (depending on your state), grandparents day, Easter break/spring break, field trips, and the list goes on and on. These changes can really challenging for some students, so try to stay grounded, and keep your routines as consistent as possible. It is okay to have "fun days", but make sure you prep your classroom on what to expect, and establish rules for such days so that the chaos is somewhat organized.

Look at the school calendar to see what your schedule is going to be like during the last month of the year. Try to let the students know what is coming up, but also remind them that to participate in the fun activities. The students need to continue to work hard and follow the classroom expectations. Keep as many routines as you can in place.

DAY 147

Whoever dwells in the shelter of the Most High will rest in the shadow of the Almighty.

PSALM 91:1 NIV

Determine with your grade level team what are the critical assignments your content areas are, and let those be the ones that you take home and grade. The other assignments could be graded by the students to help provide them feedback and allow for corrections. Not every single assignment needs to go in the grade book, but you want to have enough with a balance of homework and assessments. You will want a fair representation of the student's body of work at the end of the quarter.

Sometimes, you just need to put the papers away and do something that does not involve your job for an evening. The last quarter of the year is so busy that it is hard to find some quality time with family and friends.

Make it a point to slow down a little and by enjoying your students, family, and by taking care of yourself during the last quarter. You will need to be fresh until the end of the year!

DAY 148

*Until I come, give attention to the public reading
of Scripture, to exhortation and teaching.*

1 TIMOTHY 4:13 **NIV**

T ake time to read more to your students. This is a bit harder for the secondary level because you are limited by how much time you have with your students each day. Sometimes, you may only see your students a few times a week. Read to your students if you can. No matter what age the students are, they still like to hear someone read to them. Find a novel that will resonate with your students. One book that we always read to our fifth-grade is *One for the Murphys*. This is a high-interest story with real-life problems that students may encounter.

Your librarian or media center specialist might have some good recommendations for you. If you still cannot quite find what you are looking for, go to your public library and ask for some assistance. If you can find a book that will resonate with your students, they will be hooked, and hopefully, enjoy the break for a few minutes and being able to get lost in a good book. I have always found that this is a great way to end your day if possible. Even at the secondary level, you might be able to read a few minutes during a week. I know that I remember many of the books that my teachers read to me over the years, and you could help change students lives through a story.

DAY 149

And Mary said: "My soul glorifies the Lord and my spirit rejoices in God my Savior...for the Mighty One has done great things for me—holy is his name."

LUKE 1:46–47, 49 NIV

Celebrate the little things as much as you can. The small achievements that students make over time will give them the confidence to continue to push themselves to reach their full potential. All students deserve a chance to have their success recognized, even if it is in a small way. Some students might like public recognition in front of the class, while others might like a small note on the top of their paper or in their desk. Continue to push these students to do their best work and celebrate these victories often.

Remind students of what goals they have set for themselves. Help the student keep track of their goal, and give them some affirmation for working hard to reach their goal. Encourage them to keep trying, and along the way, you will see transformations for many of your students. Set goals, track, and celebrate success!

DAY 150: REFLECTION AND PRAYER

DAY 151

"Worthy are you, our Lord and God, to receive glory and honor and power, for you created all things, and by your will they existed and were created."

REVELATION 4:11 ESV

Enjoy learning outdoors when possible. Late spring is a great time to get outdoors with your students. I am definitely a hands-on learner, and there is just something about being outside in fresh air that makes learning and teaching more fun. Students love to go outside to free read, or work on spelling words, or math facts using sidewalk chalk It is a nice change of pace from being under the fluorescent lights all day. As the days get closer to summer, everyone will want to be outside even more, so why fight the urge?

One way to get students outside more while still being productive is to purchase or borrow clipboards. Tie a string to the clipboard to hold a pencil on the other end so that students can be prepared and work on their assignments. I have found that when you tell students you are going outside to do something, they are so excited about going that they leave everything in the classroom. Be proactive as the weather becomes better, so you can enjoy some time with your students in an outdoor learning space.

DAY 152

Feed the hungry, and help those in trouble. Then your light will shine out from the darkness, and the darkness around you will be as bright as noon.

Isaiah 58:10 NLT

K now that some students look forward to the end of the year, but some do not. School is often "the safe place" for students where adults care and the students get proper nutrition. The thought of summer can be scary for those students that need structure. In many districts across the country, students and families are relying on the schools to help provide two meals a day for their child. I asked some of these students, "What do you usually do for breakfast and lunch over the summer?" Many students responded, "I don't eat breakfast, and I find some chips or something to eat at lunch, and then I usually have dinner, but not always."

Think about each of your students, and see what impact summer vacation might have on their lives. Get in contact with your social worker at school and see if there are some programs you can help your families get in touch with to access food from a local food bank, donations for personal care items, etc. What a difference you could make for a child and their family by providing them resources over the break.

DAY 153

Being confident of this, that he who began a good work in you will carry it on to completion until the day of Christ Jesus.

PHILIPPIANS 1:6 NIV

Teaching can sometimes be a thankless job. We pour so much into our students, and in 180 or so days they leave us. Oftentimes, we do not hear from these students again. This can be a little disheartening because of the amount of energy we put into our students with seemingly small returns up front. What you are doing for these students each day is invaluable. Caring for your students each day will provide huge dividends for them down the road. You may not see all the fruits of your labor, but there will be occasions in the future when you have former students come back, and tell you all of the amazing things they are doing. Know that you were a part of that.

Pour everything you have into those children and young adults even when it is not easy. God will reward you with energy, patience, and peace knowing that you have given everything you have for His children. Even if you teach in a public school, your actions and words can be a light to Christ that they may not find elsewhere.

DAY 154

You were chosen to tell about the excellent qualities of God...

1 Peter 2:9 GW

K eep in contact with your parents until the end of the school year. Conferences are a great way to help parents stay up-to-date on their child's education, but that only occurs two times a year. Keep in regular contact with them when their child is doing some great things at school as well as when students are starting to struggle. Assist parents with monitoring their child's grades, missing assignments, etc. Also, keep the parents informed regarding upcoming events, such as parent/teacher conferences.

There are a few ways to keep parents current on what is happening in your classroom and around the school. One is sending out a monthly newsletter or email to keep parents informed about relevant information for the next few weeks. Families may not have internet access at home, and their phones could be shut off, so if this is the case, it is probably better to mail the documents to their mailing address or send home them with the student. Also, make sure the document is written in the language that is spoken in the home. Hopefully, you have some great resources around you who can help translate your newsletters. This practice will ensure that you have tried to keep everyone on the same page in order to help their child finish the end of the year well.

DAY 155: REFLECTION AND PRAYER

DAY 156

Then God blessed the seventh day and made it holy, because on it he rested from all the work of creating that he had done.

GENESIS 2:3 NIV

Try not to use spring break to "catch up" on work. The work will get done. I see many teachers on the last day of school, before spring break loading up their cars with papers and curriculum binders to look at over the break. However, there might be instances when you will definitely need to catch up on your work during the break. I have always found that time away brings a sense of revitalization to work. Not checking email or grading papers is good for the soul.

This is a great time to start a new hobby or do some traveling. If you are like me in my first year, I was still paying off student loans, and making a lot of frozen pizzas, so I did not go on a fancy vacation for during those first few years. You could catch up with some old friends or meet some new ones by trying out a new restaurant. You could also attend a concert or play that you have always wanted to see. Staying out a little later during a weekday and then being able to sleep in is a fantastic feeling. You have worked hard, and you deserve it!

DAY 157

And the LORD answered me: "Write the vision; make it plain on tablets, so he may run who reads it."

HABAKKUK 2:2 ESV

The end of the year will sneak up on you quicker than you think. The third marking period seemed like it took a long time with minimal breaks and the shorter days. The activities in the fourth quarter will make it go so fast that you want to make sure that you are planning ahead for all of these activities. Ensure that you are hitting the standards you need to complete before the end of the school year.

Plan for abbreviated lessons during days when you have special events scheduled. Often, there are field days, half days, emergency drills, and field trips that have to be taken into account when planning your curriculum. It is hard to get a lot accomplished on the day of a big event, so plan on having your more involved lessons before or after days with activities and additional lessons on the days when the events will take place. I often have students absent more in the last few weeks of school, so helping students keep track of missing work and keeping parents informed will only help you at the end of the year. The more you plan ahead for the end of the year, the more you can relax and enjoy those fun events with your staff and students.

DAY 158

*So that I may come to you with joy, by God's will,
and in your company be refreshed.*

ROMANS 15:32 NIV

Relax and enjoy the weather outside to help you finish the rest of the year. One way to do this is to go to some sporting events or other activities for your students. Many of your students will be involved in spring sports such as track, baseball, softball, etc. Ask your students for a schedule and try to make it to a game or two. Your students will be so happy that you came to watch them play. This will give you some much needed time away from school work, and a chance to further your bond with some of your students.

Cabin fever, in my opinion, is a real illness. Warm weather and sunshine sure does a body good! A little yard work or hike will get your body up and moving around, and give you a little bit of a jump start.

I cannot get to the gym as much now with young children at home, but these little guys force me to get up and act like a kid again! I am incredibly blessed to have these guys as my personal trainers. I hope that you feel rejuvenated as the last few weeks of school come to a close.

DAY 159

An intelligent heart acquires knowledge,
and the ear of the wise seeks knowledge.

PROVERBS 18:15 ESV

Continuing education is always taking place in our profession. Maybe you are thinking about getting a master's degree. It may be a good time to start looking at programs and online vs. on-campus options. Take a look at your district contract and pay close attention to the pay scale. At the top from left to right, it typically runs from a bachelor's degree to somewhere around a master's +30 additional credits (MA 30) or a PhD level. Often, a pay increase will pay for the degree in a few years. It is always nice to move up the pay scale!

Most accelerated programs run around eighteen months or so. Online is an excellent option because you can still travel or work from home. As long as you have internet access, you can still complete your work. Professional development is necessary to obtain your professional license in your state, so an advanced degree helps give you a bump in pay as well as meets the criteria for your professional development.

DAY 160: REFLECTION AND PRAYER

DAY 161

But test everything; hold fast what is good.

1 THESSALONIANS 5:21 ESV

Finishing well should always be a conscious concern for a teacher coming back after spring break. When the students, many whom do not necessarily want to be there, see that you give hints at not wanting to be there either—trouble will ensue! After spring break is a great time to have students set goals for their personal and academic progress to help guide them through the rest of the year. Without some sort of direction, academic or behavior issues will begin to surface as well.

Keep up with the communication with parents. Call or email as soon as you see behaviors that are not typical for that student. This could also be a positive phone call. One student might come back from break and have a renewed sense of ownership for their learning, so you will want to call home to congratulate the student, and affirm all of the hard work. Often, there is a correlation between behaviors at home and at school. Work with the parents to help get your students back on the right path to have a successful end of the year.

DAY 162

For the word of God is alive and active. Sharper than any double-edged sword, it penetrates even to dividing soul and spirit, joints and marrow; it judges the thoughts and attitudes of the heart.

HEBREWS 4:12 NIV

If you are struggling to keep up, but are too proud to ask for help, you will continue to stress out and eventually be behind. Spend some time today in God's word and ask for strength and endurance through these last days of the year.

I am not sure what you need at this moment or what door you may need to be opened, but He does. Spending time in His word and in prayer will help you to make good decisions and stay on the path he has called you to follow. Maybe you are considering going back to school, or you just have a couple of tough students that you feel like you cannot make on your own. Ask God for patience, guidance, and the discipline to follow His will when He calls you to do so. When I have been patient and waited, I have never been led astray because it was part of His plan for me. Ask, seek, and knock regarding your concerns or decisions today, and be ready to follow Him wherever He takes you!

DAY 163

*God is working in you to help you want to do
and be able to do what pleases him.*

PHILIPPIANS 2:13 NCV

Do unexpected things for your students: act out your lesson, hold class outside, take a nature walk, help younger students, or eat lunch with students. Small surprises work too, such as no homework, treats, visit a teacher, fun projects, or students teaching each other, etc. This will make them excited for what you have planned. At this time of year, they are always up for fun, so have fun and be unpredictable. This is a great way to keep students who are frequently absent at the end of the year coming to school. This can also include preparing students for their transition to a new classroom or building next year.

Try and plan a trip to see possible teachers the students might have next year. This is especially important for the transition from elementary to middle school and from middle school to high school. There might be some students (and parents) who are very anxious about the transition to the next grade level. Help alleviate that stress by taking a trip to see the next grade level teachers at the new building. The students seem to enjoy these trips, and always have some great questions to ask their future teachers. Remind students that they are going to be leaving a first impression on their new teachers as well as administrators at their new school. Remember to hold students accountable for school-wide expectations on these school visits.

DAY 164

And we know that in all things God works for the good of those who love him, who have been called according to his purpose.

ROMANS 8:28 NIV

You will adore these children by the end of the year more than you will ever believe, and the thought of graduating them out of your room will leave an ache in your heart. Do not be ashamed of your emotions. With summer break coming up and a renewed sense of energy, you will face another group in the fall. I asked one of my veteran teacher colleagues what he liked most about teaching, he replied: "When years later you meet a former student in the mall or somewhere else, and they introduce you to their children as their favorite teacher, or share a lesson they learned from you; the long days and nights will all be worth it. It still happens to me over thirty years later."

What a great perspective this teacher has about teaching! It is difficult to lose a group of students, but you will be so proud of the gains they have made, knowing that they will be great citizens, and leaders of our country. If they leave us with a glimpse of how to treat others with respect, kindness, and grace, the academics will follow. Teach students how to love one another as God loves us, and our world will be a much better place.

DAY 165: REFLECTION AND PRAYER

DAY 166

"I am with you always, to the very end of the age."
MATTHEW 28:20 NIV

You are almost there! Keep pouring encouragement into these students before they leave for the summer. Hopefully, your state testing assessments are over and if not, keep motivating your students in any way you can to help them give their best. Reward them for their efforts by adding some extra downtime with an extra recess, less homework, time to listen to music on their device, etc. These students have a lot of pressure put on them to perform, so help them take the edge off a little bit.

Spend some time talking about what the next year will look like for your students. Some of you might teach fifth grade, so preparing students for their transition to middle school will be necessary. Secondary teachers will need to help prepare their students for the rigors of high school or college. Have a conversation with them about what the next step for them might look like, and what options are out there for them. At this age, counselors play a considerable role in setting up classes for high school students that will prepare them for what they want to do post-graduation. Keep your bar set high, but also keep it light and fun for your students. Give students who may have some anxiety about the upcoming break more of your time, so they can process their own transition to summer vacation even though it may be a few weeks away.

DAY 167

The Father has loved us so much that
we are called children of God.

1 JOHN 3:1 NCV

Teaching can be the most rewarding, yet frustrating job in the world. You cannot be doing it for the money. Over the course of the year and your career, you will have hundreds of children who have learned how to make mistakes and that they will be ok. You have taught them how to treat others well how to think, and how to work well as a team. Be proud of that. There is nothing like it in the world.

DAY 168

As each has received a gift, use it to serve one another,
as good stewards of God's varied grace...

1 PETER 4:10 ESV

Focus on the students you have reached and the lessons that have gone well. It is easy to start thinking about who still needs more support, and environmental factors that are inhibiting students from performing to the best of their ability. Thinking about this too long can start to get you down. There is so much good that has come out of this year so far. Look back at the beginning of the school year, reflect on how much your students have grown. They are not perfect by any means, but they are improving, and so are you! Think back to that first week of school and how scattered you were just trying to keep your head above water. You may still be trying to keep your head above water, but now you have the tools to help keep you afloat.

It is often humbling to think about your lessons that did not go well, and some blunders that occurred along the way. You have learned so much from your students, colleagues, and parents about the student population in which you serve each day. Take some time to reflect on some positive changes in your classroom. This time of year can be hard because some of your toughest students (which are never absent by the way), continue to test and challenge you each day. Pray for strength, perseverance, and guidance to help reach these students. Your hard work is paying off!

DAY 169

A time to weep, and a time to laugh;
a time to mourn, and a time to dance...

ECCLESIASTES 3:4 ESV

Find time for yourself. When I started teaching, I was at school for twelve plus hours each day. I would work through my lunch break, and then work several hours on the weekend. Some people (like me) enjoy the daily hustle, and would rather spend the time getting things done rather than have a to-do list hanging over their heads. That is fine, just make sure you find time for yourself. Understand that those twelve-hour days should be temporary, or you will burn out. Do some yoga, plan a weekend getaway, go for a run, do SOMETHING other than school work. Although being a teacher is a part of who you are, it should not be **all** that you are.

At this point in the year, you may have lost contact with some of your friends during this first or second semesters of teaching. If you recently graduated from college, many of your friends are probably in the same boat as you. Everyone is working hard on their careers and starting their life after college. Try to reach out to some of your friends to see how their careers are going. It will be nice to catch up and hear about experiences as well. Although many of you might have different career paths, many of your experiences may be similar, and you can relate to one another. Plus, it is just great to catch up with an old friend.

DAY 170: REFLECTION AND PRAYER

DAY 171

*Seek God's kingdom, and all the other things
you need will be given to you.*

LUKE 12:31 NCV

Dream big and take action. Now that you have almost a year under your belt, where do you see yourself going in the next few years? Do you want to pursue another degree, work with other children in your community during the summer, or take a mission trip to help others in need? Whatever your passions may be for this summer or the following school year, pray about them and give them to God. He knows your heart, and if you are willing to follow Him and do His will, then he will open more doors than you ever thought possible.

I am always amazed by how God has been at work in my life since I started teaching. He has placed colleagues and students in my life at just the right time to help me to become a better teacher, husband, father, and man because of the relationships and experiences I have had in education. If you are willing to let His plan to work out in your life, you will become a better teacher and person because you are emulating the best teacher there ever was in Jesus Christ.

DAY 172

And the effect of righteousness will be peace, and the result of righteousness, quietness and trust forever.

ISAIAH 32:17 ESV

Find some time in your day to be still. This can be hard to do as a teacher. There is always something to do when your students are in the room; and a lot of preparation to accomplish when your students are not in your classroom. I find this problematic myself, but when I make time to slow down, I have found that it helps me to gain perspective, relax, and to give an opportunity for God to speak truth into my life.

There are some times in the day when it is easier to take a minute or two and just be still. I have found that early in the morning, before the kids wake up, works best for me. I have also found that during lunch can be a good time, especially if the morning was difficult and you need to reset before the afternoon begins. It is so important to spend some time in reflection and reading God's word. This is one area that I need to continue to work on and make it a priority in my life. When I do, everything else seems to fall into place for me because I am following the plan God has for me.

DAY 173

"Listen to this, Job; stop and consider God's wonders. Do you know how God controls the clouds and makes his lightning flash? Do you know how the clouds hang poised, those wonders of him who has perfect knowledge?"

JOB 37:14–16 NIV

Find a way to bring the outdoors to your classroom. In the spring, there are signs everywhere of God's creation waking up from its winter rest. Help your students see God's creation up close and personal by exposing them to it. There are many ways you can incorporate this in your classroom. Science class is probably one of the most available avenues in which to bring nature into the classroom. Nature can also be incorporated in other subject areas, such as math, language arts, and social studies.

If you search "outdoor activities for your classroom" in a search engine, I am sure you will locate more results than you need. I have always enjoyed having my students write their journal entries outside during a language arts lesson, and focus on something they could see around them in nature. The assignment for them was to zoom in on an aspect of nature around them, and write a story about what they saw. Have fun with these activities, but remember to have a backup plan in case it starts to rain.

DAY 174

I always thank my God for you because of his grace given you in Christ Jesus. For in him you have been enriched in every way—with all kinds of speech and with all knowledge...

1 CORINTHIANS 1:4–5 NIV

Ask students for feedback on how to improve your classes for next year. Students are usually pretty honest about your performance. Granted, you will have a few students who say it is cruel and unusual punishment to have homework any night of the week, but look for nuggets of feedback that will help you in that second and third year of teaching. Even though I have been in the profession for a while, I still look forward to the feedback, and I try to use that feedback to adjust how I teach in the classroom.

Setting up a survey can be as high or low tech as you want it to be. An example of a survey with more technology would be utilizing a product like Survey Monkey or Google forms. These types of web-based applications allow you to see who responded ,or you could make it anonymous. A low-tech option would be creating a few questions for students on a piece of paper and having them write down aspects of your teaching that you did well, and areas that need improvement. Have them describe what they have enjoyed about your class, and what was a struggle for them. Hold on to this feedback, and look back at it again at the start of the next year when you are planning for the new school year. You will find that this feedback will help you refine your craft of teaching.

DAY 175: REFLECTION AND PRAYER

DAY 176

Therefore, if anyone is in Christ, he is a new creation; old things have passed away; behold, all things have become new.

2 CORINTHIANS 5:17 NKJV

Remember, every year is a new year, and you get a fresh start. As this year comes to a close, take a closer look at how your year went. Celebrate all of the growth you and your students have made. Think about some of the trials and speed bumps along the way with learning new curriculum, grading, school policies, and teaching your students. You have come a long way! Throughout the year, you have been shaped and molded into the person and teacher that God wants you to become. You have stuck with it, and next year you will be that much more ahead of the learning curve.

Maybe you had a rough time this year: your students might have been very challenging; colleagues were not as supportive as you had hoped; or maybe you had personal issues on your mind during the school year. There will always be hard times in teaching. You might have experienced all three of those issues this year, and thought that this was not the way teaching would turn out for you. Seek God for guidance, strength, and faith in knowing that He has been at work in your life. Lean on Him and not your own understanding, and know that you will have some rest to recharge and knowledge to work through some of the challenges from this year.

DAY 177

God is not unjust; he will not forget your work and the love you have shown him as you have helped his people and continue to help them.

HEBREWS 6:10 NIV

B e an advocate for your students and your school when out in the community. I overhear conversations all the time when someone asks a person how their job is going, and they respond with negative issues that are happening in their workplace. It is easy to focus on the negative aspects of what might be going on, but also try and be the light for your school and the children that you work with. For every issue that your school has, I am hopeful that you have three to four positive stories that you can share with others.

This summer and next fall, talk with others in the community about activities and other events that are happening at the school. I often hear that parents feel disconnected from the schools once their child has moved on to the next grade level, because they are no longer getting those monthly or weekly newsletters. Many people in the community want to be involved, whether that is attending an event, volunteering, or fundraising. Give these folks a chance to get involved by being the voice of the great things that are happening in your building and community.

DAY 178

May the God who gives endurance and encouragement give you the same attitude of mind toward each other that Christ Jesus had, so that with one mind and one voice you may glorify the God and Father of our Lord Jesus Christ.

ROMANS 15:5–6 NIV

Take the summer to reflect and refine what worked and eliminate what did not work. Hopefully, throughout the year, you have made notes during some great lessons that you want to try again next year. There will definitely be some lessons you wish you had an extra day for remediation or enrichment. Take a couple of days this summer to see where you might be able to fit this into your curriculum for next year. Talk to your colleagues, and they might be having similar thoughts. Work together to produce a scope and sequence that allows the best outcomes for student learning.

This summer, visit your local library or go online to find a good book just to read for personal enjoyment as well as book to build your skillset around curriculum, instruction, and/or behavior management. Learn how to assist those with physical, emotional, and developmental challenges that you might have in your classroom next year. You might already have a class list for next year at this point. If so, begin to check in with their current teacher(s) to better understand who your future students are, as you release your own students for the summer.

DAY 179

"It is finished."
JOHN 19:30 NIV

I t's official! You have completed your first year. Way to go! This is a fantastic time for you, and a big relief knowing that all of that hard work, energy, prayer, and self-sacrifice has helped to shape some exceptional individuals this school year. On this last day of school, spend some meaningful time with your students reflecting on some experiences you had together as a group. These end-of-the-year activities are helpful for students as many of them may not see a lot of their classmates over the summer. Have fun and enjoy the last few hours with your students. Walk them to the bus and give them a high five on the way out the door. They deserve a break as well!

For the remainder of the afternoon, once students have left, remember to pack up things that you may want to take home over the summer. I label everything with my name and room number on it as many schools do a big cleaning over the summer. This may mean that your classroom materials may end up in the hallway for some time before the cleaning is finished. Take some time to visit with your colleagues, custodians, and administrators before you leave for the summer. Thank them for all of the support and encouragement they have given you over the year. It takes a village to teach a student, and often a community to groom a teacher! Well done this year. Take time to recharge, relax, and thank God for such a great year!

DAY 180: FINAL REFLECTION / GOALS FOR NEXT YEAR

_____

_____

_____

_____

_____

_____

_____

_____

_____

_____

_____

_____

_____

_____

_____

_____

_____

_____

_____

_____

_____

_____

About the Author

Tyler Harms attended Calvin College, where he earned a bachelor's degree in special education and elementary education. He has two master's degrees in both special education and mathematics. Tyler has been advocating and serving students, families, and other educators for over a decade. He has served as a special educator in both elementary and secondary schools.  He often coaches student teachers and new educators as they navigate their first year of teaching. Tyler enjoys being in the outdoors fishing, hiking, hunting, and simply enjoying nature with his family. Tyler resides in West Michigan with his wife and their three boys along with their fun-loving lab, Rocky.

www.teachforgodsglory.com
Teaching For God's Glory
@teachingforgodsglory